7 Simple Steps
to
Salvation

Larry D. Harper

The
Elijah
Project

Mesquite, Texas

7 Simple Steps to Salvation
© 1995, 2010, 2012 by The Elijah Project
New Matter © 2009, 2010, 2012 by The Elijah Project
Mesquite, Texas

ISBN: 978-1-880761-09-0

Portions of the contents previously published as "What's Left of the
Right That Stayed Down When He Went Up," *The Voice of Elijah Update*,
September 1995.

Translations of the writings of Irenæus and Hippolytus were taken from
The Ante-Nicene Fathers, edited by Alexander Roberts and James
Donaldson (Edinburgh, 1886).

Address all correspondence to:
The Elijah Project
P.O. Box 870153
Mesquite, Texas 75150

Printed in the United States of America.

CONTENTS

WHAT'S LEFT OF THE RIGHT
THAT STAYED DOWN
WHEN HE WENT UP?[1]

Introduction

As of this past August 17th,[2] it has been twenty-nine years since God called me; and I have spent that entire time asking Him what He called me to do. I'm still asking, folks, but I'm not getting any more specific answers concerning the what, when, and how of my calling today than I did back then. I am a lot more comfortable saying, "I don't know" than I used to be. I am also more confident of what I do know and more willing to admit I've made some serious mistakes. One thing I know for certain is, I can see that Satan has "sown" a whole lot of "tares" in God's Church.[3] Those "tares" manifest themselves as the lies Satan has managed to "plant" in the Church and the people who firmly believe them.

Twenty-one years ago[4] I was forced to face the fact that the only way I could ever fulfill the calling God had placed on my life was to root out all the lies I believed at that time. To do that, I realized I had to aggressively question the traditional understanding of the biblical message that one finds in the Church today and be willing to reject anything that did not agree with the little bit of insight I had at that time. So I packed up all the theology class notes I had taken in college and seminary and set out on a personal odyssey in search of God's Truth. Since that time I have so rigorously challenged the things I have heard in the Church that at times I have wondered how Christian tradition could possibly have anything at all to contribute to the Truth.

---

[1] This book contains a reprint of an article titled "What's Left of the Right That Stayed Down When He Went Up?" in *The Voice of Elijah Update*, September 1995.

[2] This is referring to August 17, 1995.

[3] Matthew 13:24–30.

[4] This is referring to April 1974.

Well, folks, I have recently come full circle and now find myself right back where I was twenty-nine years ago when God called me. I now understand the only accurate information the Church gave me was what I needed to know to be born again. That is, it gave me the basic Truth concerning salvation by faith.[5] Other than that, it has given me little that Satan has not, in some way or other, twisted into a lie.

This time around, however, I am not the only one I know who has experienced the absolutely phenomenal transformation that accompanies the new birth. I now have people around me that I am absolutely certain have had the same born-again experience that I had when I was twelve years old. That does not bode well for all those Pretenders in the Church who want to go on pretending all is well with their souls.

The further we go in this endeavor, the more born-again Believers are going to come together. When we compare notes concerning our salvation experience, we are going to find we have all had exactly the same life-transforming encounter with the Almighty God. That will make it rather easy for us to spot a Pretender who wants to go on ignorantly pretending some emotional experience or other qualifies him to be called a child of God. Pretenders may not know who they are because they prefer to go on believing Satan's lie; but born-again Believers will know what Pretenders don't know. And when the time comes for the "grain" to be "winnowed" in the "wind," the few remaining bits of "chaff" among us will be carried away. You can trust me on that one. When Jesus Christ returns for His Own, God will have His Church waiting, "without spot or wrinkle."[6]

It amuses me a bit when I hear recent converts *talk about* the miracle they *received* as a result of their encounter with the Lord of Glory. I get the feeling they sort of went to God expecting to be forgiven and then go on about their lives pretty much as usual. It doesn't happen that way, folks. If you have ever been born again, you will know it beyond a shadow of any doubt. Satan may have been extraordinarily successful selling "easy-believism" to morons over the past several decades, but that doesn't change the stone-cold facts. As the Apostle Paul said:

> *Therefore if any man is in Christ, {he is} a new creature; the old things passed away; behold, new things have come.*
> (2 Corinthians 5:17)

It is impossible for anyone to have the salvation experience Paul is describing in that verse and not be certain something absolutely incredible

---

[5] When I use the term *faith*, I am using it with the sense of WHAT *one believes* rather than with the ridiculous sense of THAT *one believes*. Everyone believes something about God, but WHAT *one believes* in that regard is what matters.

[6] Ephesians 5:27.

has happened to them. Contrary to popular opinion, the new-birth experience is not something that happens and you don't feel anything. When you have been born again, you don't have to be encouraged to believe you have been. *You know it.* So don't let the agents of Satan convince you otherwise. The new birth radically reorders your entire existence. The person you are after the new birth is not the person you were before.

Let me encourage you with this admonition: If you want all that God has to offer, don't stop with asking for His forgiveness. Ask for the gift of His Holy Spirit.[7] Keep asking until He grants your request. Hell will be filled with sinners who experienced God's forgiveness and then went back to living in sin. Only the children of God are going to Heaven. And the only way to become a child of God is to be born again. That simply *means* the Holy Spirit has to come in and do a top-to-bottom remake of the person you have been. So don't let some ignorant "christian" who has made some goofy "confession of faith" talk you into settling for anything less.

So What's New With You?

For the past twenty-one years I have been consumed by a desire to know the full extent of God's Truth. Over the years, the message of the Hebrew Scriptures (actually there are seven separate messages hidden there) has gradually become a lot clearer to me. Since 1981, however, I have known that God did not call me to teach unbelievers the things I understand.

The problem was, at that time, I had no idea how to distinguish a True Believer from a Pretender. If you've been reading what I've written over the past five years[8] and listening to what I've recorded, you know I've had a hard time getting a handle on that one. But believe me when I tell you, God has ways to teach even a numskull like me. Fourteen years is a long time to cover the same ground time after time, but I think I have finally gotten the point. Pretenders act in accordance with some lie that they believe. True Believers act like children of God because they believe the Truth. That's a rather simple truism. It just took a whole lot of learning on my part. You know, "Stupid is as stupid does."

Over the past year, I have at long last come to understand why the things I see in Scripture were never *meant* for the ears of anyone who is not a true child of God. I can see now that unbelievers will never appreciate the value of the Truth because they cannot fully comprehend it. You see, the things God called me to teach are, as Paul said, "foolishness" to the one who has not been born again:

---

[7] Luke 11:5–13.

[8] From 1990 to 1995.

*For Christ did not send me to baptize, but to preach the gospel, not in cleverness of speech, that the cross of Christ should not be made void. **For the word of the cross is to those who are perishing foolishness, but to us who are being saved it is the power of God.***
(1 Corinthians 1:17–18)

Now, I fudged a bit in using that verse. Paul is not talking generally about *The Teaching* when he mentions "the gospel" and "the word of the cross." He is *talking* specifically *about* the things one needs to believe in order to be born again. But the same thing can be said about *The Teaching* I have been called to teach born-again Believers. So I just took what Paul said about "the gospel" and applied it to *The Teaching*. I knew he wouldn't mind.

The distinction I just made between "the gospel" and *The Teaching* is an appropriate segue into the things I intend to explain in this book. I want to tell you why God called me as a Teacher and has somehow seen to it that I am now working every day to *restore The Teaching*. In the process I will provide you a bit of basic background information that you must understand before you can fully appreciate why the loss of *The Apostolic Teaching* around A.D. 200 was no great catastrophe as far as God is concerned. As a matter of fact, it was exactly what He knew would happen all along. Therefore, Satan's success in orchestrating the loss of *The Apostolic Teaching* played right into God's hand. But before you can understand what God has been accomplishing in the Church over the past eighteen hundred years, you must first understand the nature of the four offices of the Church that God "calls" individuals to fill.

The Calling of God

If you have been around the Church for any length of time at all, I'm sure you have heard lots of folks say, "God called me *into the ministry.*" That is a lie. Although those folks may fervently believe that what they have said is true, it is a lie nonetheless. They may feel "called," but I'm not *talking about feelings.* I'm *talking about* the supernatural calling of God. God has not called, and never will call, anyone "*into the ministry.*" That is because God only calls people to fill one of the four offices of the Church. He always has, and He always will. So if one of those whom God actually has called doesn't know which of the four offices God called him to fill, I have no doubt he misunderstood his "calling."

Perhaps you are already aware of the passage where Paul describes the offices God calls men to fill:

But to each one of us grace was given according to the measure of Christ's gift. Therefore it says,

"WHEN HE ASCENDED ON HIGH,
HE LED CAPTIVE A HOST OF CAPTIVES,
AND HE GAVE GIFTS TO MEN."

(Now this {expression,} "He ascended," what does it mean except that He also had descended into the lower parts of the earth? He who descended is Himself also He who ascended far above all the heavens, that He might fill all things.) And **He gave some {as} apostles, and some {as} prophets, and some {as} evangelists, and some {as} pastors and teachers, for the equipping of the saints for the work of service,** *to the building up of the body of Christ; until we all attain to the unity of the faith, and of the knowledge of the Son of God, to a mature man, to the measure of the stature which belongs to the fulness of Christ.*
(Ephesians 4:7–13)

That passage rather straightforwardly lists the four offices of the Church: (1) the Apostle, (2) the Prophet, (3) the Evangelist, and (4) the Pastor/Teacher. The "pastors and teachers" designation applies to only one office. Paul added the term *pastor* to bring the *parabolic imagery* of the Prophets to the mind of the reader. The English term *pastor* does not even accurately represent the *parabolic imagery* that stands behind the term. The Greek text *literally* says "shepherds." Paul's point is, the one who occupies the office of the Teacher is supposed to impart his knowledge of *The Teaching* to the Lord's "flock" in order to protect God's "sheep" from "wolves"—that is, from false apostles, prophets, and teachers. I could explain the *parabolic image* of the "shepherd" in more detail, but that is part of *The Teaching*—and is not relevant in this context. The following statements of Jesus and Paul will have to do for now:

"Beware of the false prophets, who come to you in sheep's clothing, but inwardly are ravenous wolves."
(Matthew 7:15)

"Behold, I send you out as sheep in the midst of wolves; therefore be shrewd as serpents, and innocent as doves."
(Matthew 10:16)

"Go your ways; behold, I send you out as lambs in the midst of wolves."
(Luke 10:3)

"I am the good shepherd; the good shepherd lays down His life for the sheep. He who is a hireling, and not a shepherd, who is not the owner of the sheep, beholds the wolf coming, and leaves the sheep, and flees, and the wolf snatches them, and scatters {them.}"
(John 10:11–12)

"I know that after my departure savage wolves will come in among you, not sparing the flock."
(*Acts 20:29*)

When we *talk about* God's "calling," we are actually *talking about* the "right" He has conferred on certain individuals to minister in, or for the benefit of, His Church. "Right" is just another way of saying "authority." So let's *talk* a bit *about* the authority attached to each of the four offices. Paul has given us a ranking of the authority of the three highest offices of the Church in the first of his letters to the church at Corinth:

And God has appointed in the church, first apostles, second prophets, third teachers, then miracles, then gifts of healings, helps, administrations, {various} kinds of tongues. FOUR OFFICES OF AUTHORITY PLACED
(*1 Corinthians 12:28*) ON EARTH BY GOD. JESUS.
— MAIN FOCUS —

In that passage Paul is *talking about* the fact that, in the Early Church, each office in the Church came with a different authority, depending on the message the individual had been called or appointed to preach. However, the unifying purpose that tied all of the offices together was "the building up of the body of Christ."[9] Incidentally, in that phrase, the verb "build up" should be translated as just "build." Paul is alluding to the *parabolic image* of "building" God's "house" by fitting together the "living stones" that Peter mentions in 1 Peter 2:5. But you probably already knew that.

The Evangelist

I'll begin by explaining the authority of the Evangelist. Paul mentioned only the Apostle, Prophet, and Teacher in his letter to the Corinthians because he was *talking about* the three offices that minister directly to Believers *inside the Church*. An Evangelist had (and still has) no authority whatsoever minister to True Believers. His calling was (and still is) to convert sinners, not to instruct Believers. So the limits of his authority restricted him (and still restrict him) to preaching "the Gospel"—that is, to preaching the message of salvation by *faith*—so that sinners might escape the wrath of God. He preached that salvation message *outside the Church*, because—in contrast to the situation in the Church today—that's where all the unbelievers were.

You can get some idea of the role the Evangelist played in the Early Church by studying the activities of Philip, whom Luke specifically called an "evangelist"[10]:

---

[9] Ephesians 4:12, 16. See also Acts 20:32; Romans 14:19; 2 Corinthians 10:8, 13:10; 1 Thessalonians 5:11; Jude 1:20.

[10] Acts 21:8.

*But Saul {began} ravaging the church, entering house after house; and dragging off men and women, he would put them in prison. Therefore, those who had been scattered went about preaching the word. **And Philip went down to the city of Samaria and {began} proclaiming Christ to them.** And the multitudes with one accord were giving attention to what was said by Philip, as they heard and saw the signs which he was performing. For {in the case of} many who had unclean spirits, they were coming out {of them} shouting with a loud voice; and many who had been paralyzed and lame were healed. And there was much rejoicing in that city. Now there was a certain man named Simon, who formerly was practicing magic in the city, and astonishing the people of Samaria, claiming to be someone great; and they all, from smallest to greatest, were giving attention to him, saying, "This man is what is called the Great Power of God." And they were giving him attention because he had for a long time astonished them with his magic arts. But **when they believed Philip preaching the good news about the kingdom of God and the name of Jesus Christ,** they were being baptized, men and women alike. And even Simon himself believed; and after being baptized, he continued on with Philip; and as he observed signs and great miracles taking place, he was constantly amazed.*
(Acts 8:3–13)

But an angel of the Lord spoke to Philip saying, "Arise and go south to the road that descends from Jerusalem to Gaza." (This is a desert {road}.) And he arose and went; and behold, there was an Ethiopian eunuch, a court official of Candace, queen of the Ethiopians, who was in charge of all her treasure; and he had come to Jerusalem to worship. And he was returning and sitting in his chariot, and was reading the prophet Isaiah. And the Spirit said to Philip, "Go up and join this chariot." And when Philip had run up, he heard him reading Isaiah the prophet, and said, "Do you understand what you are reading?" And he said, "Well, how could I, unless someone guides me?" And he invited Philip to come up and sit with him. Now the passage of Scripture which he was reading was this:

"HE WAS LED AS A SHEEP TO SLAUGHTER;
AND AS A LAMB BEFORE ITS SHEARER IS SILENT,
SO HE DOES NOT OPEN HIS MOUTH.
IN HUMILIATION HIS JUDGMENT WAS TAKEN AWAY;
WHO SHALL RELATE HIS GENERATION?
FOR HIS LIFE IS REMOVED FROM THE EARTH."

*And the eunuch answered Philip and said, "Please {tell me}, of whom does the prophet say this? Of himself, or of someone else?" **And Philip opened his mouth, and beginning from this Scripture he preached Jesus to him.** And as they went along the road they came to some water; and the eunuch said, "Look! Water! What prevents me from being baptized?" [And Philip said, "If you believe with all your heart, you may." And he answered and said, "I believe that Jesus Christ is the Son*

of God."] And he ordered the chariot to stop; and they both went down into the water, Philip as well as the eunuch; and he baptized him. And when they came up out of the water, the Spirit of the Lord snatched Philip away; and the eunuch saw him no more, but went on his way rejoicing. But Philip found himself at Azotus; and as he passed through he kept preaching the gospel to all the cities, until he came to Caesarea.
(Acts 8:26–40)

It is obvious from those passages that Philip was ministering as an Evangelist, preaching "the Gospel" message of salvation by *faith* to unbelievers *outside the Church*. Thousands of Evangelists have done exactly the same thing down through the centuries. Did you hear what I said? Although Protestants prefer to believe otherwise, the Roman Catholic Church never completely lost "the Gospel"—that is, the salvation message concerning Jesus Christ. God has always had Evangelists working in one area of the Church or the other, even during the darkest hours of the Dark Ages.

The last major summons that God issued to Evangelists appears to have been during the 1940s and 1950s. At that time, several such men of God began to fulfill their calling, with a few of them eventually carrying "the Gospel" message of salvation by *faith* around the world. Only when they failed to remain within the bounds of the limited authority they had *received* from God—the authority to preach "the Gospel" to unbelievers *outside the Church*—did they fall short of what God sought to accomplish through them.

The Teacher

In contrast to an Evangelist, who was either called or appointed to preach "the Gospel" to unbelievers *outside the Church*, a Teacher was called or appointed to minister only to True Believers *inside the Church*. As a matter of fact, the Teacher's calling prohibited him from teaching unbelievers. Hence, Early Christians were sometimes accused of being a secret society with secret rituals when, in fact, Early Church Teachers were merely trying to fulfill their calling in accordance with the authority attached to their office.

A Teacher also had the authority to teach "the Gospel," but that was only because *The Teaching* includes a detailed explanation of the salvation work Jesus Christ accomplished. The Teacher's purpose in teaching "the Gospel" was not to convert sinners, however, it was to instruct True Believers.

The office of Teacher was intended to be nothing less than a continuation of the teacher/disciple relationship that existed between Jesus and His disciples. That is, a Teacher was supposed to *hand down* to his disciples *The Teaching* that Jesus Christ *revealed* to the Apostles after His Resurrection.[11] He

---

[11] Luke 24:44–45.

was to teach them *The Mystery* God had hidden in the Hebrew Scriptures. Of the teacher/disciple relationship, Jesus said this:

"A pupil is not above his teacher; but everyone, after he has been fully trained, will be like his teacher."
(Luke 6:40)

That is why the writer of the Book of Hebrews chastised his readers for not being diligent disciples of the Truth:

*For though **by this time you ought to be teachers**, you have need again for some-one to teach you the elementary principles of the oracles of God, and you have come to need milk and not solid food.*
(Hebrews 5:12)

That verse leaves the firm impression that everyone could become a Teacher. To a certain extent, that was true. As we will see later, an Apostle, Prophet, or Teacher could appoint anyone to the office of Teacher, and God would honor their calling to that office as long as they taught the Truth they had *received*. James, on the other hand, said this:

Let not many {of you} become teachers, *my brethren, knowing that as such we shall incur a stricter judgment.*
(James 3:1)

James' warning was not heeded. The Church lost *The Apostolic Teaching* because more than a few imbeciles were extremely eager to be Teachers, but had no desire at all to protect the integrity of the things they were taught. Paul *talked about* those kinds of people in his first letter to Timothy:

*As I urged you upon my departure for Macedonia, remain on at Ephesus, in order that you may instruct certain men not to teach strange doctrines, nor to pay atten-tion to myths and endless genealogies, which give rise to mere speculation rather than {furthering} the administration of God which is by faith. But the goal of our instruction is love from a pure heart and a good conscience and a sincere faith. **For some men, straying from these things, have turned aside to fruitless discus-sion, wanting to be teachers of the Law, even though they do not understand either what they are saying or the matters about which they make confident assertions.***
(1 Timothy 1:3–7)

Obviously, for *The Apostolic Teaching* to be lost, the office of Teacher must have eventually been occupied by individuals who did not even bother learning the *oral tradition* the Church was supposed to be **handing down** from generation to generation. Instead of teaching what they had been taught, they did what the Apostle Peter knew they would. They taught whatever sounded good to them:

*But false prophets also arose among the people, just as **there will also be false** **teachers among you, who will secretly introduce destructive heresies,** even denying the Master who bought them, bringing swift destruction upon themselves.*
(2 Peter 2:1)

Consequently, the situation we face in the Church today is exactly what the Apostle Paul described to Timothy:

For the time will come when they will not endure sound doctrine; but {wanting} to have their ears tickled, they will accumulate for themselves teachers in accordance to their own desires; and will turn away their ears from the truth, and will turn aside to myths.
(2 Timothy 4:3–4)

The one thing you must keep in mind concerning the office of Teacher is this: Since the loss of *The Apostolic Teaching*, there has been nothing for a Teacher to teach. Hence, God has not, until our own time, had any reason to call a Teacher. That is because anyone called to be a Teacher would have to first *restore The Apostolic Teaching* before he would have anything at all to teach True Believers. As you well know, I claim to be doing just that. You can believe that if you care to. You can disbelieve it if you dare to. What you do one way or the other won't change the fact that I am going to do exactly what God has called me to do. And every last one of the Redeemed of the Lord is going to hear the Truth that God has called me to teach. That Truth will prepare them for what is yet to come. You can go to hell if you so choose. But I have absolved myself of all complicity in your case because I have told you the Truth concerning your situation just as my calling demands.

The Prophet

The Prophet in the Early Church had the specific authority of God to warn Believers concerning future events that demanded their immediate attention so that they could take the necessary precautions. The revelation these men were given had nothing to do with *The Apostolic Teaching*. It had to do with everyday circumstances. That is easy to see from the following two passages where mention is made of the prophetic ministry in the Book of Acts:

Now at this time some prophets came down from Jerusalem to Antioch. And one of them named Agabus stood up and {began} to indicate by the Spirit that there would certainly be a great famine all over the world. And this took place in the {reign} of Claudius.
(Acts 11:27–28)

And as we were staying there for some days, a certain prophet named Agabus came down from Judea. And coming to us, he took Paul's belt and bound his own feet and hands, and said, "This is what the Holy Spirit says: 'In this way the Jews at Jerusalem will bind the man who owns this belt and deliver him into the hands of the Gentiles.'"
(Acts 21:10–11)

Prophets continued ministering in the Church until at least the beginning of the fifth century. References to their ministry can be found scattered throughout the literature of the Early Church. No less a figure than the renowned theologian St. Augustine admits he knew an individual—St. John of Egypt—who accurately predicted future events in his own day (A.D. 400).[12]

The problem God faced in continuing to call Prophets was one of constituency. To whom was He to send a Prophet after the Church became coextensive with the state? When that happened, there was, for all intents and purposes, no longer any clearly defined group of Believers to warn. Hence, with the exception of a few instances scattered down through the centuries, all mention of the prophetic ministry ceased within a century after the secularization of the Church under Constantine.[13]

The Apostle

The office of Apostle came with the complete authority of Jesus Christ Himself. That is, an Apostle had the authority to do whatever it took to get the job done. His was the authority of Prophet, Teacher, and Evangelist all rolled up into one. He could preach to the lost, teach the Redeemed, and warn Believers concerning future events. As we have already seen, Peter and Paul both functioned as Prophets when they warned the Church concerning the loss of *The Apostolic Teaching.*

However, an Apostle also had the authority to establish local churches and settle disputes between Believers. That went well beyond the combined authority of the Prophet, Teacher, and Evangelist. The authority attached to those three offices inhered completely in the right to speak or not to speak as they so chose. That is, they could do just as Jesus said:

"And whoever does not receive you, nor heed your words, as you go out of that house or that city, shake off the dust of your feet."
(Matthew 10:14)

---

[12] See Augustine, "Care for the Dead," Chap. 17, *The Fathers of the Church,* Ed. Deferrari, Washington, D.C.: The Catholic University of America Press, 1955.

[13] See "How the West Became 'Christian': Constantine and the Church," *The Voice of Elijah,* July 1994.

It isn't entirely obvious from the following passage, but the authority Jesus transferred to His disciples shortly before He ascended was the authority to teach the things—the *oral tradition*—He had taught them, and to do whatever was necessary to ensure that *oral tradition* was **handed down** from generation to generation in the Church:

> *And Jesus came up and spoke to them, saying, "All authority has been given to Me in heaven and on earth. **Go therefore and make disciples of all the nations, baptizing them in the name of the Father and the Son and the Holy Spirit, teaching them to observe all that I commanded you;** and lo, I am with you always, even to the end of the age."*
> *(Matthew 28:18–20)*

The apostolic authority was absolute. That is what Jesus *meant* when He said, "All authority has been given to Me in heaven and on earth. Go therefore and …." He was giving His disciples the "right" to act on His behalf. They were to take His authority and use it to accomplish the task He sent them to accomplish. Not only did their authority as Apostles *mean* they could make decisions as if they were Jesus Christ Himself, Jesus also promised them their actions would be honored as if they were His Own—that is, He would be with them—provided they adhered to the *oral tradition* they had **received**. That *meant* they had authority to appoint others—that is, "call" them as Jesus did the Apostle Paul—to the various offices of the Church. That is exactly what the Apostles did in the following passage:[14]

> *Now at this time while the disciples were increasing {in number,} a complaint arose on the part of the Hellenistic {Jews} against the {native} Hebrews, because **their widows were being overlooked in the daily serving** {of food.} And the twelve summoned the congregation of the disciples and said, **"It is not desirable for us to neglect the word of God in order to serve tables.** But select from among you, brethren, seven men of good reputation, full of the Spirit and of wisdom, whom we may put in charge of this task. But we will devote ourselves to prayer, and to the ministry of the word." And the statement found approval with the whole congregation; and they chose Stephen, a man full of faith and of the Holy Spirit, and Philip, Prochorus, Nicanor, Timon, Parmenas and Nicolas, a proselyte from Antioch. **And these they brought before the apostles; and after praying, they laid their hands on them.***
> *(Acts 6:1–6)*

You can read Luke's account in the Book of Acts for yourself and see that two of those appointed by the Apostles at that time—Stephen and Philip—

---

[14] Few scholars have understood the actions described in this passage because Luke spoke *parabolically* concerning the "daily serving" and the Apostles spoke *parabolically* when they said "serve tables."

immediately went out preaching the Gospel as Evangelists. That is because the Apostles appointed them to that office when they laid hands on them. You can also see that the leaders of the church at Antioch followed the same practice of laying on hands when they elevated Barnabas to the office of Apostle at the direction of the Holy Spirit:

> Now there were at Antioch, in the church that was {there}, prophets and teachers: Barnabas, and Simeon who was called Niger, and Lucius of Cyrene, and Manaen who had been brought up with Herod the tetrarch, and Saul. And while they were ministering to the Lord and fasting, the Holy Spirit said, "Set apart for Me Barnabas and Saul for the work to which I have called them." Then, when they had fasted and prayed and laid their hands on them, they sent them away. (Acts 13:1–3)

Later on, Luke lets us know Barnabas had been appointed an Apostle by calling both Paul and Barnabas "apostles":

> But when **the apostles, Barnabas and Paul,** heard of it, they tore their robes and rushed out into the crowd, crying out and saying, "Men, why are you doing these things? We are also men of the same nature as you, and preach the gospel to you in order that you should turn from these vain things to a living God, WHO MADE THE HEAVEN AND THE EARTH AND THE SEA, AND ALL THAT IS IN THEM." (Acts 14:14–15)

On the basis of these passages we can safely assume the Apostles must have laid hands on Matthias when they appointed him to replace Judas Iscariot.[15] My point is, the eleven Apostles understood the authority Jesus Christ gave them in Galilee was exactly the same authority the Pope claims to have today. In the absence of God sovereignly calling someone, as He did the Apostle Paul, the Apostles knew they could lay hands on anyone and appoint them to fill the offices of the Church. Paul mentions that authority in connection with Timothy's "calling" by the "elders":

> Do not neglect the spiritual gift within you, which was bestowed upon you through prophetic utterance with the laying on of hands by the presbytery. (1 Timothy 4:14)

We know that Timothy was appointed to at least the office of Evangelist because Paul mentions that specifically:

> But you, be sober in all things, endure hardship, **do the work of an evangelist,** fulfill your ministry. (2 Timothy 4:5)

---

[15] Acts 1:15–26.

Paul also lets us know Timothy was a Teacher with the authority to appoint others as Teachers:

> *And the things which you have heard from me in the presence of many witnesses, these **entrust to faithful men, who will be able to teach others also.***
> (2 Timothy 2:2)

The cumulative effect of Paul's statements is to tell us the "elders" most likely laid hands on Timothy in order to appoint him as an Apostle. I say that because Paul repeatedly admonished Timothy concerning his responsibility in regard to disciplining Believers. The activities he mentions—evangelizing, teaching, and disciplining Believers—make sense only if Timothy was an Apostle. That also fits in with the fact that Paul warns Timothy not to be too hasty in his appointment of others to positions of authority in the Church:

> *Do not lay hands upon anyone {too} hastily and thus share {responsibility for} the sins of others; keep yourself free from sin.*
> (1 Timothy 5:22)

In a couple of places in his second letter to the Corinthians, Paul alludes to the absolute authority he had as an Apostle to discipline Believers:

> *For even if I should boast somewhat further about our authority, which the Lord gave for building you up and not for destroying you, I shall not be put to shame, for I do not wish to seem as if I would terrify you by my letters.*
> (2 Corinthians 10:8–9)

> *For this reason I am writing these things while absent, in order that when present I may not use severity, in accordance with the authority which the Lord gave me, for building up and not for tearing down.*
> (2 Corinthians 13:10)

Did you notice he mentioned "building" in both of those passages? He had in mind the purpose for which God called men to fill the four offices of the Church. You can see that purpose clearly in what he said concerning the ministry of the Apostles, Prophets, Evangelists, and Teachers in Ephesians:

> *And **He gave some {as} apostles, and some {as} prophets, and some {as} evangelists, and some {as} pastors and teachers, for the equipping of the saints for the work of service, to the building up of the body of Christ;** until we all attain to the unity of the faith, and of the knowledge of the Son of God, to a mature man, to the measure of the stature which belongs to the fulness of Christ.*
> (Ephesians 4:11–13)

The point of that passage is not only that God called men to various offices for the purpose of "building" His Church, but also that those men carried out their calling so the Church could "attain the unity of the *faith*" and "the *knowledge* of the Son of God." Paul doesn't tell us that purpose could only be accomplished if those appointed to the offices of the Church (whether by God Himself or by His legitimate representative) understood both the limits of their authority and the message they were supposed to preach. So let's talk a bit about that.

What's It All About, Anyway?

The Truth concerning the ministry and authority of the four offices of the Church has been obscured by what Catholic Church leaders did to contribute to the loss of *The Apostolic Teaching*. They took three general terms that can be found in the New Testament writings and in the apostolic literature—*bishop, presbyter,* and *deacon*—and applied them to a rigid Church hierarchy of appointed offices that left little room at all for the sovereign calling of God.

What Church leaders did can be seen by comparing the apostolic work titled "The Teaching of the Twelve Apostles" with a revised copy of the work that first saw the light of day sometime after *The Apostolic Teaching* was lost.[16] The revision omits an entire section concerning the proper respect to be accorded Apostles, Prophets, and Teachers. In the remaining text, all mention of these three offices has been replaced by "bishops," "presbyters," and "deacons."

The Truth is, the three terms *bishop, presbyter,* and *deacon* are not specific titles. They are general terms used to designate a characteristic of someone who ministered to the Church in any one of a variety of functions. You can get some idea of how the terms are used if you take a look at what they actually *mean*. The term bishop *means* nothing more than "overseer" or "guardian." That is reflected in its use as a description of Jesus Himself:

> For you were continually straying like sheep, but now you have returned to the Shepherd and **Guardian** of your souls.
> (1 Peter 2:25)

The same is true of the term *presbyter*. It refers to an older person, that is, an "elder." That is apparent from the fact that it is used in the New Testament with reference to the Jews:

> And when He had come into the temple, the chief priests and the **elders** of the people came to Him as He was teaching, and said, "By what authority are You doing these things, and who gave You this authority?"
> (Matthew 21:23)

---

[16] Compare "The Teaching of the Twelve Apostles" with "Constitutions of the Holy Apostles" Vol. VII of *The Ante-Nicene Fathers*, Ed. A. Cleveland Coxe, 1886.

The term *deacon* stands up no better under scrutiny. It turns out to *mean* nothing more than "servant" or "one who serves." That should be obvious from the way Jesus used the term:

> *"And do not be called leaders; for One is your Leader, {that is,} Christ. But the greatest among you shall be your **servant**."*
> *(Matthew 23:10–11)*

If you need more evidence, consider the fact that Paul called both himself and Apollos "deacons":

> *What then is Apollos? And what is Paul? **Servants** through whom you believed, even as the Lord gave {opportunity} to each one.*
> *(1 Corinthians 3:5)*

You can see from this how Satan enticed Church leaders into using the three terms *bishop*, *presbyter*, and *deacon* to stifle the dynamic ministry of God's Apostles, Prophets, and Teachers. He did that to shift the focus of Church leaders away from *The Apostolic Teaching* and center it on the human administration of the Church. More recently, he has used those terms as a red herring to head off anyone who would seek to continue the Protestant search for what the Early Church had and the Roman Catholic Church lost—that is, anyone who would continue the search for Truth that was initiated by the leaders of the Protestant Reformation.

You see, when the Protestant Church broke off from the Roman Catholic Church, Protestant leaders claimed the authority of Scripture as their sole authority. They did that to counter-balance the apostolic authority the Roman Catholic Church claimed for the Pope.[17] While the Protestant claim may seem fine in theory, it left the practical side of Protestant Christianity with a huge hole in it. It was rather easy for Roman Catholics to know they were in submission to the authority of the Pope. If they accepted the papal decrees, they had submitted to the papal authority.

Protestants soon discovered submission to the authority of Scripture was another matter entirely. It was difficult, if not impossible, to demonstrate submission to the authority of Scripture when the pronouncements of Scripture had to be *interpreted* before they could even be understood. The vexing question then became, "Whose *interpretation* of Scripture is authoritative and worthy of our submission?" Thus began the Protestants' futile search for some scholar (or scholars) who, like the Pope, could make an authoritative declaration as to what the Scriptures had said. Half a thousand denominations, sects and splinter groups later, most Protestants today have come to the conclusion that one person's *interpretation* of Scripture is just as

---

[17] See "The Protestant Confession: The Church Lost *The Teaching*," *The Voice of Elijah*, January 1992.

good as another's. Thus the Protestant search for Truth has finally been sacrificed at the altar of the priesthood of the Believer.

Not long after the Protestant Reformation began, however, it dawned on Protestant leaders that Believers didn't have to submit to any authority as long as one person's *interpretation* of the Scriptures was just as valid as that of everyone else. So they set out to recreate the governmental structure of the Early Church, thinking the problem they faced lay in the fact that the Roman Catholic Church had lost that as well as the Truth concerning salvation by *faith*. That is why the Protestants now have Episcopalian, Presbyterian, and Congregational forms of government, to name but a few. Each new Protestant form of government arose out of a claim that it most nearly represented the original Early Church form of government. However, each one—with a few notable exceptions—was based on Satan's lie concerning Scripture's use of the three terms *bishop*, *presbyter*, and *deacon*.

Protestants were on the right track when they appealed to the authority of Scripture and the priesthood of the Believer. However, they failed to factor in the four offices to which God calls individuals, the apostolic authority inherent in the Gospel and *The Apostolic Teaching*, the Church's loss of *The Apostolic Teaching* and the fact that, without revelation, nobody could gain access to the message of the Hebrew Scriptures because it had been sealed.

Nevertheless, Protestants were right on the mark in rejecting the authority of the Pope. They somehow sensed the Truth that, after the Church lost *The Apostolic Teaching*, one Pope could pass along his authority to the next Pope in an unending chain of pious Popes until hell freezes over. That would never change the fact that the apostolic authority inheres only in the *oral tradition **handed down*** by the Apostles. So, echoing the sentiment of the leaders of the Protestant Reformation, I have but one more thing to say concerning the apostolic authority of the Pope: "Sorry, Mr. Pompous Pope Pious the Umpteenth, you may have *received* a legitimate appointment to your office, but you didn't *receive* the Truth, so you have absolutely no authority in the sight of God."

Granted that the Pope has no authority, but where did the Reformation leave the Protestant Church? It left it in essentially the same limbo as the Roman Catholic Church. You see, the Reformers *restored* only the Gospel—that is, the Truth concerning salvation by *faith*. That Truth is still taught as a fundamental part of Protestant theology to this day. But the only authority God ever attached to that specific message is the authority an Evangelist has to preach salvation by *faith outside the Church to unbelievers*. Therefore, Protestants have had no more authority to teach Believers than the Roman Catholic Church from which they broke away. The authority to teach *Believers*—that is, the authority attached to the office of Teacher—inheres in *The Apostolic Teaching*, and that *oral tradition* was lost around A.D. 200. According to the plan of God, it has remained completely hidden in the Hebrew Scriptures until our own day when, in the wisdom of God, True Believers will once again understand the complete Truth of *The Apostolic Teaching*.

Did you understand what I just said? The Protestant Reformation was nothing more than a clarification and widespread distribution of the Gospel message of salvation by *faith*. The Reformers were able to *restore* that Truth to its rightful place at the center of the (Protestant) Church because that is the message one finds in the New Testament. In contrast to *The Apostolic Teaching*—that is, the message of the Hebrew Scriptures—the Gospel message of the New Testament was never sealed. It has been available to anyone who wanted to understand and respond to that little bit of Truth. That is why every generation of the Church has had those few True Believers who experienced the reality of the new birth.

Over the last several decades, the Protestant Church has seen the fundamental Truth of the Gospel distorted by agents of Satan who teach ignorant doctrines that do nothing more than deceive. Yet it is still possible for a person to be born again, provided they hear the Truth from an Evangelist who has *received* a legitimate calling or appointment to preach the Gospel. As we draw nearer the End, that circumstance is becoming increasingly more unlikely.

Let me say one final thing concerning the office of Evangelist. Some of the various "soul-winning" ministries in the Church today have authority to do what they are doing; others don't. The reason for that is quite simple. God has called thousands of Evangelists down through the centuries. Some have *handed down* to others both the Gospel they were called to preach and their authority to preach that message. So there are undoubtedly thousands of people in the Church today who have *received* a legitimate authority to preach the Gospel. Unfortunately, there are millions of others who have no authority whatsoever in that regard.

The first problem with the unhappy circumstance the Church faces today is this: It is not always easy for a person to confirm that they have *received* a legitimate authority to preach the Gospel. If they were authorized to do so by an Evangelist whom God called directly or by an Evangelist who was authorized by an Evangelist whom God called, etc., they have authority to preach the Gospel. If they weren't, they don't. As you can see, if you are not a first-generation Evangelist—that is, if you did not *receive* a supernatural call from God yourself—tracing your evangelistic "roots" is an "iffy" proposition. How would you know for sure?

However, the second problem related to the authority one has to preach the Gospel today is even more insidious. I have repeatedly told you the authority of the four offices of the Church inheres in the message preached. That being the case, if "the gospel" a legitimate Evangelist preaches has been seriously distorted to the point where it does not contain the essentials necessary for one to be born again, that Evangelist has no authority to preach that "gospel." Moreover, he is no longer an Evangelist of God; he has become an agent of Satan!

Under the circumstances I have just outlined, I would not advise anyone to engage in "soul winning" unless they are absolutely certain they have *received* a supernatural call from God Himself. Trust me on this one. You may not always be able to tell the difference between the two, but God has His Evangelists working right alongside the agents of Satan. Let them do their job. Be content to do what God has "called" you to do. Believe me, if you are a True Believer, you have an "authority." I'll tell you about it later.

An Exercise in Futility? Hardly.

After the Church lost *The Apostolic Teaching*, a long line of Popes continued to *hand down* what many consider to be the apostolic authority Jesus gave to His disciples. They have been ignorantly conducting an exercise in futility. The authority of Jesus Christ inheres completely in the message He *handed down* to His disciples—that is, in *The Apostolic Teaching*. Without an accurate understanding of that original message, the Roman Catholic Church has been involved in nothing more than pomp and circumstance. That brings us to the point where we must ask the question: What has God accomplished in the Church since the loss of *The Apostolic Teaching* 1800 years ago?

If the only Truth available since the Church lost *The Apostolic Teaching* has been the Gospel message of salvation by *faith*, what has God been doing down through the centuries? He has been doing exactly what He did before *The Apostolic Teaching* was lost. He has been testing True Believers to see whether or not they will continue to hold on to the Truth they believe and refuse to believe a lie. You see, your salvation is not determined by how much Truth you have, but whether you live according to the Truth you understand. Under those circumstances, you can be saved by believing only the bare essentials necessary to be born again, provided you continue to live according to that Truth. I didn't say that; Jesus did:

> *"And that slave who knew his master's will and did not get ready or act in accord with his will, shall receive many lashes, but the one who did not know {it,} and committed deeds worthy of a flogging, will receive but few. And from everyone who has been given much shall much be required; and to whom they entrusted much, of him they will ask all the more."*
> (Luke 12:47–48)

Now, as long as the Early Church understood *The Apostolic Teaching*, True Believers did their best to exclude Pretenders and continually strive to live in perfect obedience to the Truth they heard taught in the Church. Under those conditions, God often tested His Church by allowing it to endure horrible persecution. His testing accomplished two extremely valuable goals: (1) it purged every last Pretender from the portion of the Church that endured testing, and (2) it allowed True Believers to reach even higher levels in their walk with God. I didn't say that, a man who went through a few of those persecutions did:

> For what is the issue of persecution, what other result comes of it, but the approving and rejecting of faith, in regard to which the Lord will certainly sift His people? **Persecution, by means of which one is declared either approved or rejected, is just the judgment of the Lord. But the judging properly belongs to God alone. This is that fan which even now cleanses the Lord's threshing floor— the Church, I mean—winnowing the mixed heap of believers, and separating the grain of the martyrs from the chaff of the deniers; and this is also the ladder of which Jacob dreams, on which are seen, some mounting up to higher places, and others going down to lower. So, too, persecution may be viewed as a contest.** By whom is the conflict proclaimed, but by Him by whom the crown and the rewards are offered? You find in the Revelation its edict, setting forth the rewards by which He incites to victory—those, above all, whose is the distinction of conquering in persecution, in very deed contending in their victorious struggle not against flesh and blood, but against spirits of wickedness. So, too, you will see that the adjudging of the contest belongs to the same glorious One, as umpire, who calls us to the prize. **The one great thing in persecution is the promotion of the glory of God, as He tries and casts away, lays on and takes off.** But what concerns the glory of God will surely come to pass by His will. And when is trust in God more strong, than when there is a greater fear of Him, and when persecution breaks out? The Church is awe-struck. Then is faith both more zealous in preparation, and better disciplined in fasts, and meetings, and prayers, and lowliness, in brotherly-kindness and love, in holiness and temperance. There is no room, in fact, for ought but fear and hope. **So even by this very thing we have it clearly proved that persecution, improving as it does the servants of God, cannot be imputed to the devil.**[18]

That just about tells the tale concerning persecution. The Early Church understood its function, and True Believers accepted it as an opportunity to prove their firm belief in the Truth they understood. They could readily see that it purged Pretenders from among them, and they agreed with that objective. The problem is, after Church leaders began to readmit those who had denied the Truth during persecution, the Church was never again the domain of True Believers alone. Therefore, the first of God's purposes in allowing persecution was lost.

---

[18] Tertullian, *De Fuga in Persecutione, I.*

With the readmission of those who had denied the *faith*, the Body of Christ lost the purity it had gained during the persecution and immediately became a mixture of True Believers and infidels. When that happened, Satan had not only successfully "sown tares" in God's Church,[19] he had also gotten them to grow. Pretenders changed the Church completely. Within a century after the Church began to routinely readmit Pretenders who denied the *faith* during persecution, Christianity became the official religion of the state, and persecution of Christians ceased.

So how has God been testing True Believers since the visible Church ceased to be the exclusive residence of God's children? That's rather easy to see once you understand the Church lost *The Apostolic Teaching*. He has been using Satan's lies to accomplish His Own ends. Remember I told you the Gospel has always been available? Well, everyone who has ever been born again by believing the Gospel has immediately gone looking for more Truth. Just as immediately they have been confronted by the lies that Satan has sown in God's Church. The test has always been, "Will you continue to believe the Truth of the Gospel, or will you distort it by believing a lie that allows you to go back on the commitment you made when you were born again?"

It hasn't helped that True Believers have had a difficult time seeing through the pretense of Pretenders. They rather naïvely assume everybody in the Church has experienced the same inner transformation they experienced when they were born again. That has made it easy for God to use Pretenders to test True Believers with their careless living, to see whether True Believers will go back to believing a lie that allows them to do the same things Pretenders do.

God's test has been made doubly difficult by the limited amount of Truth that has been available to True Believers since the loss of *The Apostolic Teaching*. The only thing that True Believers have had to help them withstand the test posed by Pretenders and the lies of Satan has been their limited knowledge of the Truth of the Gospel message they believed when they were born again.

In some ways, the testing True Believers have been made to endure since Pretenders took over the Church has been even more brutal than the cruel persecutions Early Church Believers had to endure. If it seems that way to you, cheer up. As the Early Church Father Irenæus knew all too well, God is going to put us all to the test one last time during the reign of the Antichrist. Irenæus called that "the last contest of the righteous."[20] But just remember how he concluded that sentence: "in which, when they overcome, they are crowned with incorruption."

---

[19] Matthew 13:24–30.

[20] See *The Advent of Christ and AntiChrist*, p. 75.

That tremendous opportunity for demonstrating your love of the Truth won't appear until we have done our best to exclude all those who love Satan's lies more than the Truth. In the meantime, you need to get the picture firmly in your mind. Over the past thirty or forty years, millions of people around the world have been born again under the ministry of Evangelists God called to preach the Gospel message of salvation by *faith outside the Church*. In the wisdom of God, those True Believers immediately went back into the Church seeking more Truth. Little did they know they had been called to withstand God's ultimate test.

Born-again Believers are right now being tested by some of the most insidious "tares" (lies and liars) that Satan has ever "sown" in God's Church. Consequently, some have long since given up the Truth they understood when they were born again. Giving in to Satan's onslaught, they have instead found comfort and refuge in a lie. However, there are still True Believers out there searching for Truth. Those folks still have a chance, provided they hear the Truth and believe it before it's too late.

I have been called as a Teacher to make available the Truth of *The Teaching* to those born-again Believers who are still seeking Truth, and I make absolutely no apologies for my calling. However, God has called me to teach only those who "love the truth."[21] I have nothing to say to anyone who rejects any part of what I teach. To tell the Truth, I am supposed to, and will, encourage them along "their way." I certainly don't have the time or any inclination to argue with them. As a matter of fact, Scripture tells me I should not do that:

> *Do not speak in the hearing of a fool,*
> *For he will despise the wisdom of your words.*
> (Proverbs 23:9)

We are still a few years away from the time when large numbers of True Believers will respond to the Truth I have to teach. In the meantime, I must put together lots of information for their consumption. So far, it's coming together rather well. I have good reason to believe that trend will continue.

So Where to From Here?

I have repeatedly stated that I do not claim to be an Apostle; I do not claim to be a Prophet; and I do not claim to be an Evangelist. I claim that God called me as a Teacher. What I have stated in the past was true at the time. However, recent events have changed my circumstances somewhat. I now have the authority of an Evangelist. How so? Well, in the wisdom of God and, apparently, according to His unique plan, I stole it from someone

---

[21] 2 Thessalonians 2:10.

who didn't know he had it and, as best as I could tell, either wasn't willing or didn't know how to use it.

The story of how I came to be an Evangelist begins nearly thirty years ago, about two weeks after God called me as a Teacher. At that time, I enrolled in a small fundamentalist Bible School where all the theology courses were taught by one man. Although some may consider that a negative, by the time that school year was over, I had a firm grasp on mainstream evangelical/fundamentalist Christian doctrine—that is, salvation by *faith*, the authority of the Scriptures, the priesthood of the Believer, and the basics of dispensational and covenant theology. I firmly believed the things I had been taught because: (1) they confirmed my new-birth experience, and (2) I was convinced God wanted me at that school to prepare for what He had called me to do.

The difficulty with what I was taught in that first year after God called me did not surface until about eight years later, when I was attending a major evangelical seminary, studying exactly the same things and hearing basically the same doctrines taught by several different men. Then I began to see that the things I had been and was being taught (other than those related to the doctrine of salvation by *faith*) were a most severe impediment to my understanding the Truth of the Scriptures. To some degree that still remains true today. That stands to reason, however, since I have already told you that nobody in the Church has any authority to teach anything other than salvation by faith. But that's another matter, so let me get back to my story.

Recently,[22] I read a short biography describing the ministry of the individual who taught me theology during that first year after God called me. In it I saw the possibility that God had called him as an Evangelist. On a hunch, and desperate to find someone whom I felt confident: (1) had been called to preach the Gospel to unbelievers; and (2) had not seriously distorted that salvation message by adding Satan's lies to it, I contacted my mentor from years ago.

My intuition concerning the man's calling proved correct. He told me he had been given a vision in early 1950 in which he saw millions of people being herded off a precipice to their death. All were dressed in native dress from around the world. Along with that vision he *received* his calling, "I want you to preach the Gospel to these people."

I could identify with the man's description of the vision he saw when he was called. It was a lot like the one I had when God called me. However, I soon realized he had no idea God had called him to be an Evangelist. He kept saying God had called him "into the ministry." It was obvious to me "the Gospel" referred to in his calling *meant* the message of salvation by *faith* and the people he saw in the vision were lost souls around the world. Yet I

---

[22] This is referring to early 1995.

could tell this man had never bothered to ask God what his calling *meant*. Nevertheless, over a period of three days, I brought seven people to him so that he could explain to them the message of salvation by *faith*. He confirmed He had the authority of an Evangelist when some of those people were supernaturally born again. That is a surprisingly high rate of return according to the writings of the great Evangelist Charles Finney.

Those who were born again after hearing this man explain the message of salvation by *faith* could easily see he possessed an incredible gift of God in his ability to preach the Gospel. However, I could just as easily see by the arrogant, self-righteous way he conducted himself that he had probably been using that gift to gratify himself rather than to see to it that lost souls were saved. It was obvious that, as long as he focused on the Truth of the Gospel, the calling of God gave him a confidence and eloquence he did not naturally possess. When he drifted away from that message into digressions, which he did much too often, he spoke haltingly and uncertainly. Although he obviously enjoyed preaching his own thoughts more than the Gospel, the Truth he presented was nevertheless effective for some of those who heard it.

The story does not end there, however. Over the next week, I sent other people to the good Evangelist, people who knew they had never been born again and were urgently wanting to hear a legitimate salvation message, not the goofiness that is widely available everywhere in the Church today. That's when the man proved himself to be completely unworthy of his calling. Rather than explaining God's plan of salvation so that these folks might also believe and be saved, he told them nothing about salvation by *faith*. He merely encouraged them to "confess" that they were saved—that is, to live the life of a Pretender. In other words, he demonstrated himself to be an unwitting agent of Satan.

Those who had already been born again after hearing this man preach the message of salvation by *faith* were astounded that he would ever do such a thing. I wasn't. I know full well the power that Satan wields through the lies he has spread throughout the Church. But the continued affection that those who were born again have for the man is understandable in light of what he has given them. How would you feel toward someone who had just provided you access to an incredible treasure?

The results of my recent encounter with my former teacher have surprised even me. I realize now that I have repeatedly overstepped the bounds of my authority as a Teacher in the past by trying to tell unbelievers how to be saved. I also realize how inept I was at the task of evangelizing after seeing how easily an individual called to be an Evangelist (although he had no idea such was the case) could lead a seeking soul to Christ. Along those same lines, I now realize the difficulty I have had in ridding myself of

Satan's lies is due in large part to the fact that this man overstepped the bounds of his authority as an Evangelist by teaching me things other than the fundamental message of salvation by *faith* nearly thirty years ago.

The most astounding result of the events I have just recounted is the fact that (in the wisdom of God) I stole the calling of Evangelist from this man. That unusual set of circumstances came about because I did not (as later events proved I should not) trust him to do what God had called him to do. After asking him outright whether he would lay hands on someone I sent to him and give them the authority he had as an Evangelist, I realized the straightforward approach would get me nowhere.

Not only did he not realize God had called him as an Evangelist, he (like a lot of other deluded folks out there) thought everybody has the "right" to be a "soul-winner." In spite of that belief, he was not willing to humor me in my rather unorthodox view and lay hands on anyone to give them the authority to do what he believed they already had the authority to do! Figure out that nonsense if you can! I have to my satisfaction. It's due to contention and stubbornness.

Given the fact that this man would not share an authority he didn't know he had and didn't even believe existed, I had no alternative but to entice him into doing what he would not do willingly. So I sent someone to him, ostensibly for salvation, but also with instructions to ask him one specific question: "I felt I had been called into the ministry back in the 70s. Would you pray with me asking God that I would be able to explain the message of salvation to others as you do?"

The good Evangelist readily acquiesced to that request in the presence of witnesses, thereby transferring his authority to preach the Gospel to the man I had sent. That fellow, in turn, transferred that authority to me.[23] Although my actions were certainly a bit duplicitous, I'm sure God understands. After all, Jacob got away with it, didn't he? Why shouldn't I? I have every reason to believe it was in God's plan that I discovered the man had been called as an Evangelist. Since everything else apparently went according to God's plan, why not this as well?

I have told you the foregoing to explain why I can now lay out God's plan of salvation for you. Having the Truth of the Gospel available, you can then examine yourself to see whether you have been born again. If you determine such is not the case, you will have the information necessary to decide whether you want to take the steps required to remedy that unfortunate situation.

---

[23] Several years later, I realized the man had already transferred his authority as an Evangelist to me nearly 40 years earlier. He did so as part of an assignment in "soul-winning" during a course on evangelism.

The Word of the Cross

The Apostle Paul has this to say concerning the Truth one must believe in order to be born again:

For the word of the cross is to those who are perishing foolishness, but to us who are being saved it is the power of God. For it is written,

"I WILL DESTROY THE WISDOM OF THE WISE,
AND THE CLEVERNESS OF THE CLEVER I WILL SET ASIDE."

*Where is the wise man? Where is the scribe? Where is the debater of this age? Has not God made foolish the wisdom of the world? For since in the wisdom of God the world through its wisdom did not {come to} know God, **God was well-pleased through the foolishness of the message preached to save those who believe.** For indeed Jews ask for signs, and Greeks search for wisdom; but we preach Christ crucified, to Jews a stumbling block, and to Gentiles foolishness, but to those who are the called, both Jews and Greeks, Christ the power of God and the wisdom of God. Because the foolishness of God is wiser than men, and the weakness of God is stronger than men.*
(1 Corinthians 1:18–25)

As Paul indicates in this passage, the salvation message is an explanation of the Person and work of Jesus Christ. But it also includes an understanding of the rights and responsibilities of a child of God. If you have never heard an adequate explanation of the obligation you must accept as a participant in the New Covenant, I can tell you outright you have never been born again. Salvation is by *faith*. That is *faith* in the sense of WHAT *you believe*, not *faith* in the sense of THAT *you believe*. *Faith* must always have a **content**. Although I will grant that the **content** of saving *faith* can be quite minimal, it must nevertheless contain certain essential elements other than the rudimentary belief that God will forgive your sins.

Jesus Christ died on the cross to provide a sacrifice for your sins and mine. While that may seem to be a rather simple concept, the hows, whys, and wherefores of God's plan of salvation tend to get a bit more complex than the simplistic clichés that "christians" understand today. For example, there are various kinds of sacrifices described in the Hebrew Scriptures, each with its own specific purpose. Not every one of those sacrifices was a sacrifice for sin. Some were communal offerings, others were gifts. Therein lies the potential for Satan to distort the simple Truth of the Gospel message.

Since the only things in the Gospel that you need to hear and believe to be born again are those things that God requires for you to come up with the appropriate response, I'll refrain from explaining the more intricate details of the salvation message until you are able to fully appreciate them.

What I explain here are only those things you must understand before you can see through Satan's lies and respond to the Truth.

Satan's most effective distortion of the Gospel message is the widely touted "truth" that "God loves you." The very fact that you see that slogan plastered all over the place and hear the vilest of sinners spouting off about it as though it applies to them as well should tell you it is Satan's lie. It is, however, an extremely clever lie in that it is nothing more than a subtle twist on the Truth. I'll tell you more about that twist a little later.

For now you must understand that the Truth is somewhat other than "God loves you." You see, the Scriptures tell us Jesus Christ died as a sacrifice to deliver sinners from the penalty of sin that God imposed in His wrath. That is what the Apostle Paul is *talking about* in the following:

> *And just as they did not see fit to acknowledge God any longer, God gave them over to a depraved mind, to do those things which are not proper, being filled with all unrighteousness, wickedness, greed, evil; full of envy, murder, strife, deceit, malice; {they are} gossips, slanderers, haters of God, insolent, arrogant, boastful, inventors of evil, disobedient to parents, without understanding, untrustworthy, unloving, unmerciful; and, although they know the ordinance of God, that **those who practice such things are worthy of death,** they not only do the same, but also give hearty approval to those who practice them. Therefore you are without excuse, every man {of you} who passes judgment, for in that you judge another, you condemn yourself; for you who judge practice the same things. And **we know that the judgment of God rightly falls upon those who practice such things.** And do you suppose this, O man, when you pass judgment upon those who practice such things and do the same {yourself,} that you will escape the judgment of God? Or **do you think lightly of the riches of His kindness and forbearance and patience, not knowing that the kindness of God leads you to repentance? But because of your stubbornness and unrepentant heart you are storing up wrath for yourself in the day of wrath and revelation of the righteous judgment of God, who** WILL RENDER TO EVERY MAN ACCORDING TO HIS DEEDS.*
> *(Romans 1:28–2:6)*

In that passage Paul plainly *talks about* the judgment of God and the wrath He has stored up for all who stubbornly refuse to repent. In another place he tells us God's wrath is directed at all who fail to take advantage of His offer of salvation:

> *For after all it is {only} just for God to repay with affliction those who afflict you, and {to give} relief to you who are afflicted and to us as well when the Lord Jesus shall be revealed from heaven with His mighty angels in flaming fire, **dealing out retribution to those who do not know God and to those who do not obey the gospel of our Lord Jesus. And these will pay the penalty of eternal destruc-***

tion, away from the presence of the Lord and from the glory of His power.
(2 Thessalonians 1:6–9)

Pay attention to what Paul has said in that passage. "Eternal destruction" awaits those "who do not know God" and "do not obey the gospel of our Lord Jesus." I hardly think God would destroy anyone if He loved them unconditionally. I wouldn't, and I'm only a sinful human. But let's go on to see how this lie of Satan unwinds. Now, I realize fools have taken the following verse out of context to preach the lie that "God loves you," so let's take a closer look at it:

*"For **God so loved the world,** that He gave His only begotten Son, that whoever believes in Him should not perish, but have eternal life."*
(John 3:16)

Any ignorant pronouncement concerning God's love for *individual* sinners that is based on this verse can hardly stand up under closer scrutiny. The "world" that Jesus mentions refers to the totality of God's Creation here on planet Earth. It certainly does not refer to *individuals*. Keep in mind also that, in the same breath where He mentions the love God has for His Creation, Jesus has alluded to the fact that those who don't believe the message of salvation will "perish." Then take a look at the verses that immediately follow that verse:

*"For God did not send the Son into the world to judge the world, but that the world should be saved through Him. He who believes in Him is not judged; **he who does not believe has been judged already, because he has not believed in the name of the only begotten Son of God. And this is the judgment, that the light is come into the world, and men loved the darkness rather than the light; for their deeds were evil. For everyone who does evil hates the light, and does not come to the light, lest his deeds should be exposed.** But he who practices the truth comes to the light, that his deeds may be manifested as having been wrought in God."*
(John 3:17–21)

The statements Jesus made in that passage agree with what Paul told us concerning the fact that sinners are already standing under the judgment God imposed in His wrath. The Truth is, everybody alive here on Earth has already been judged and sentenced to death for committing capital crimes against God. We are all in prison, doing time on death row, awaiting execution. That is the simple message of the New Testament. Anyone who tells you differently is a liar, either ignorantly or by choice.

How could a God Who unconditionally loves every *individual* ever bring Himself to destroy them? Well, the Truth is, God does not love everybody *individually,* either unconditionally or otherwise. He loves only *Corporate*

Israel, His Firstborn Son. He hates *individual* sinners, no matter whether they are a member of Israel or not. The Psalmist has stated that plainly:

The Lord tests the righteous and the wicked,
And the one who loves violence His soul hates.
Upon the wicked He will rain snares;
Fire and brimstone and burning wind will be the portion of their cup.
(Psalm 11:5–6)

In His mercy, God has tested each one of us *individually* by offering us a pardon. If we refuse to accept His offer of salvation, we have a bit of a problem. But that is so only because the wrath of God continues to be focused directly on us:

*"Know therefore that the Lord your God, He is God, the faithful God, who keeps His covenant and His lovingkindness to a thousandth generation with those who love Him and keep His commandments; but **repays those who hate Him to their faces, to destroy them; He will not delay with him who hates Him, He will repay him to his face."***
(Deuteronomy 7:9–10)

In other words, God lets each one of us determine for ourselves whether or not He hates us. Although God has already judged us and sentenced us to death, because of His goodness, kindness, and mercy (love had nothing to do with it), He has provided the plan of salvation as a means of escape for all who will **believe** the Truth concerning what He has done for them. If people *choose* not to **believe** that Truth, they have no other way to avoid God's wrath. That is what the writer of the Book of Hebrews is *talking about* in this passage:

*For this reason **we must pay much closer attention to what we have heard, lest we drift away {from it.}** For if the word spoken through angels proved unalterable, and every transgression and disobedience received a just recompense, **how shall we escape if we neglect so great a salvation?***
(Hebrews 2:1–3a)

Some will use the following verse to tell you God must love us all *individually* because he desires that everyone repent and avail themselves of the opportunity He has provided. However, anyone who uses the verse as evidence that God loves *individuals* is ignoring the basic distinction the New Testament intentionally draws between God the Father and Jesus Christ the Son. While I will admit that distinction is, at its heart, *parabolic* in nature, it is nevertheless crucial to our understanding of what God has done. As I will explain later, the title "Lord" refers to Jesus Christ the Son. It does not refer to God the Father:

The Lord is not slow about His promise, as some count slowness, but is patient toward you, not wishing for any to perish but for all to come to repentance.
(2 Peter 3:9)

I must emphasize again that God has offered *individual* sinners a way to avoid His wrath only because of His goodness, kindness, and mercy. If His love for them had anything to do with it, they would have no hope whatsoever. But to understand why that is, you must understand the *parabolic* distinction the New Testament makes between God the Father and Jesus Christ the Son.

You see, Satan has played a shell game with this generation of "christians." Think about this for a bit. Don't you feel somewhat strange sometimes when I *talk about* "God" instead of "Jesus Christ"? By that I *mean*, isn't the mere mention of "God" considered somewhat unacceptable in "christian" circles today? The only time it is perfectly acceptable to *talk about* God as an Individual with Whom you must concern yourself is when you are *talking about* God in the abstract or in the trite statement "God loves you." That's because Satan has taken the characteristics of Jesus Christ, including the love Jesus Christ, as a man, had for sinners, and attributed them to God. He has done that because He wants to portray God as a patsy, as someone you can walk all over and never have to worry about retaliation.

Satan knows you will never respond to God honestly until you are confronted with the Truth concerning Who He actually is. Therefore I suggest you take a look at the description of God you find in the Hebrew Scriptures, keeping in mind the fact that God never changes. The Truth is, God is a jealous, vengeful God Who quite often becomes angry with those who fail to respond appropriately to His overtures of peace.

Contrary to the lie that Satan would have you believe, God the Father is not subject to *The Law of Moses*—as Jesus Christ the Son was before His death on the cross. Therefore, to attribute all the characteristics of Jesus Christ to God is folly of the first order. God hates His enemies and loves His friends. If you choose to remain an enemy of God because of your *belief* in Satan's lie, you alone are to blame for that sad circumstance. Nevertheless, I am sure unregenerate morons and others whom Satan has duped will continue to argue Satan's case in favor of the lie that "God loves you," never realizing that, when they read the following verses, they are reading someone else's mail:

*The one who does not love does not know God, for **God is love.***
(1 John 4:8)

*And we have come to know and have believed the love which God has for us. **God is love,** and the one who abides in love abides in God, and God abides in him.*
(1 John 4:16)

From the perspective of the Apostle John, who was writing to born-again Believers, the statement "God is love" describes an awesome reality that is felt by every born-again Believer. God the Father does love "us"—that is, the *Corporate* Body of Believers—with an intense love, just as the Apostle Paul has plainly stated:

> But God, being rich in mercy, because of His great love with which **He loved us**, even when we were dead in our transgressions, **made us alive** together with Christ (by grace you have been saved), and **raised us up** with Him, and **seated us** with Him in the heavenly {places}, in Christ Jesus, in order that in the ages to come He might show the surpassing riches of His grace in kindness **toward us** in Christ Jesus.
> (Ephesians 2:4–7)

The "us" in that passage refers to the entire Body of Jesus Christ. It does not refer to Believers as *individuals*. The love that God the Father has for "us" is not demonstrated to "us" as *individuals*. It is mediated through Jesus Christ the Son. According to that *parabolic imagery*, God even loved "us"—that is, the *Corporate* Body of Believers—while "we were yet sinners":

> But God demonstrates His own love toward us, in that while we were yet sinners, Christ died for us.
> (Romans 5:8)

It is of crucial importance to understand that verse is *talking about* the love that God the Father has for the *Corporate* Body of Believers—that is, for Jesus Christ, the Firstborn Son of God. It is not *talking about* His love for *individual* sinners. God does not love sinners; He hates them; and He is going to destroy them. That agrees with what Jesus Himself said:

> **"The Father loves the Son,** and has given all things into His hand. He who believes in the Son has eternal life; but **he who does not obey the Son shall not see life, but the wrath of God abides on him."**
> (John 3:35–36)

I challenge you to find any verse in Scripture that states God loved any *individual* other than Jesus Christ His Son before that *individual* entered into a covenant relationship with Him. The closest you will come is one of the verses that says something like this:

> "I have been crucified with Christ; and it is no longer I who live, but Christ lives in me; and **the {life} which I now live in the flesh I live by faith in the Son of God, who loved me, and delivered Himself up for me."**
> (Galatians 2:20)

In that verse Paul does not say God the Father "loved me." He attributes that love to Jesus Christ the Son. By contrast however, you will find Paul has stated plainly elsewhere that God did indeed hate one *individual* in particular because that *individual* despised *the Promise of God*:

> And not only this, but there was Rebekah also, when she had conceived {twins} by one man, our father Isaac; for though {the twins} were not yet born, and had not done anything good or bad, in order that God's purpose according to {His} choice might stand, not because of works, but because of Him who calls, it was said to her, "THE OLDER WILL SERVE THE YOUNGER." Just as it is written, "JACOB I LOVED, BUT ESAU I HATED."
> (Romans 9:10–13)

The reason you haven't understood that passage before (and perhaps still do not) is because the lies you have heard concerning the love of God for specific *individuals* prevent you from seeing the Truth about the hatred God has for *individual* sinners. Satan does not want people to understand this one all-important Truth: Jesus Christ the Son is the only Person of the Godhead who loves us *individually*. As Jesus Himself put it:

> "Greater love has no one than this, that one lay down his life for his friends."
> (John 15:13)

Since Jesus Christ the Son was, and still is, God, Satan has been able to use the Truth concerning His love for us to entice people into swapping the characteristics of God the Father for the characteristics of Jesus Christ the Son. But the characteristics of Jesus Christ as a man living under Law in perfect obedience to God the Father are far different than the characteristics of the Almighty God Himself.

Let me say one final thing concerning the love that Jesus Christ demonstrated by dying on the cross for each one of us *individually*. The *parabolic* distinction that exists between Jesus Christ the Son and God the Father makes perfect sense only to one who has been born again and understands the Truth concerning the parables of Scripture. For an unbeliever, it offers nothing more than an opportunity for Satan's deception. The Truth is, God the Father is an angry, jealous God who will soon take swift and total vengeance on all those who demonstrate their hatred for Him by refusing to *believe* the Truth concerning Who He is and what He has done. That includes the Truth I have just stated.

Everything Has a Price

Although, as I will explain later, the new birth is a free gift, that gift is not granted unconditionally to all. If it were, everyone would escape the wrath of God, and hell would have no purpose. That is certainly not the case. Therefore, we must carefully describe the conditions under which one can be "saved"—that is, "delivered"—from the *parabolic* kingdom of darkness (lies) and become a subject in the *parabolic* Kingdom of Light (Truth). Anyone who seeks to be born again must fulfill two requirements. They must first *repent*. Then they must *believe* the Gospel. I didn't say that, Jesus did:

> And after John had been taken into custody, Jesus came into Galilee, preaching the gospel of God, and saying, "The time is fulfilled, and the kingdom of God is at hand; *repent and believe in the gospel."*
> (Mark 1:14–15)

Although "repent and believe in the gospel" may seem simple in principle, we shall see it is somewhat more difficult in practice. We are, after all, *talking about* the salvation of individuals of whom Jesus said, "everyone who does evil hates the light, and does not come to the light, lest his deeds should be exposed."[24] While some of us may like to think that description does not apply to us, the Truth is, we are all the same. We hate the "Light" until we are born again. None of us willingly comes to God on our own; we must be drawn by the Holy Spirit. However, to compound the difficulty we have in understanding what God requires for us to be saved, the straightforward command to "repent and believe in the gospel" is stated somewhat differently in other places:

> And Peter {said} to them, **"Repent, and let each of you be baptized in the name of Jesus Christ for the forgiveness of your sins; and you shall receive the gift of the Holy Spirit."**
> (Acts 2:38)

> **"Repent therefore and return, that your sins may be wiped away,** in order that times of refreshing may come from the presence of the Lord."
> (Acts 3:19)

> "Therefore having overlooked the times of ignorance, **God is now declaring to men that all everywhere should repent, because He has fixed a day in which He will judge the world in righteousness through a Man whom He has appointed,** having furnished proof to all men by raising Him from the dead."
> (Acts 17:30–31)

Since those passages all agree that God requires repentance as the first step, let's go ahead and take a look at the role repenting plays in God's plan of salvation. Then we can go on to investigate what belief in the Gospel has to do with it. You can see from the following statement of Jesus that repentance is nothing more than the act of honestly apologizing for offenses you have committed against someone:

> "Be on your guard! **If your brother sins, rebuke him; and if he repents, forgive him.** And if he sins against you seven times a day, and returns to you seven times,

---

[24] John 3:20.

saying, 'I repent,' forgive him."
(Luke 17:3–4)

That passage tells us the object of repentance, whether to God or to your brother, is to be forgiven. However, you should keep two things in mind when apologizing to God: (1) He won't forgive if you don't willingly apologize and ask His forgiveness, and (2) He won't forgive if you don't mean it. Those conditions are not as easily met as you might think.

Before you can honestly repent, you must first understand the magnitude of your sin. By that I *mean* you must understand what God finds so completely offensive in you that He plans to destroy you. That is only possible if God sends His Holy Spirit to let you know how deeply you have offended Him. You see, God does exactly what Jesus advised us we should do in the passage above. He "rebukes" us so that we may have opportunity to "repent." Jesus described the supernatural "rebuke" (or "conviction") of the Holy Spirit in this passage:

*"But I tell you the truth, it is to your advantage that I go away; for if I do not go away, the Helper shall not come to you; but if I go, I will send Him to you. And **He, when He comes, will convict the world concerning sin, and righteousness, and judgment;** concerning sin, because they do not believe in Me; and concerning righteousness, because I go to the Father, and you no longer behold Me; and concerning judgment, because the ruler of this world has been judged."*
(John 16:7–11)

The word translated "convict" in that verse is actually a synonym for the word translated "rebuke" in Luke 17:3–4 above. You can see that from its use in the following verse:

*"And if your brother sins, go and **reprove him** in private; if he listens to you, you have won your brother."*
(Matthew 18:15)

In John 16:8, Jesus listed the three things the Holy Spirit is going to focus on when He "rebukes" you. He is going to speak to you concerning sin, righteousness, and judgment. He will first show you that your sin is unbelief—that you do not believe God has pronounced you guilty and Jesus Christ has already accomplished your salvation. Then the Holy Spirit will tell you about the righteousness of God, that He is perfectly justified in condemning you for your sin and in pardoning only those who believe the Truth. Finally, the Holy Spirit will speak to you concerning the judgment of Satan and show you that judgment applies to you just as Jesus said it did:

*"Then He will also say to those on His left, **'Depart from Me, accursed ones, into the eternal fire which has been prepared for the devil and his angels;** for I was hungry, and you gave Me {nothing} to eat; I was thirsty, and you gave Me*

nothing to drink; I was a stranger, and you did not invite Me in; naked, and you did not clothe Me; sick, and in prison, and you did not visit Me.'"
(Matthew 25:41–43)

If you have ever been rebuked by the Holy Spirit, I am certain you still remember the occasion. It is not possible for you to have endured a dressing down by the God of all Creation and not remember it. His rebuke quite literally cuts you to the quick, letting you know in no uncertain terms that you are one vile creature. So if you cannot recall ever having had such an experience, I can tell you with absolute certainty that you have never been born again. However, I can also tell you the rebuke of the Holy Spirit that provides you an opportunity for repentance will be only the first of many such rebukes, provided you respond to His first rebuke as you should. As Jesus told the church at Laodicea, He will continue to rebuke a true child of God when he/she sins so that they have continual opportunity to repent:

*"Those whom I love, I **reprove** and discipline; be zealous therefore, and repent."*
(Revelation 3:19)

The net result of what I have just told you is this: Your eternal salvation depends on the "conviction"— that is, the "rebuke"—of the Holy Spirit. That is because, until you fully understand how deeply you have offended God, you cannot honestly repent. Therefore, the Holy Spirit must rebuke you so that you understand the magnitude of your sin. He does that for everyone. It is His ministry. He will do that for you as well and, provided you are willing to accept His rebuke and repent, you can obtain God's forgiveness. That is why the Apostles *talk about* God "granting repentance":

*"He is the one whom God exalted to His right hand as a Prince and a Savior, **to grant repentance to Israel, and forgiveness of sins.**"*
(Acts 5:31)

*And when they heard this, they quieted down, and glorified God, saying, "Well then, **God has granted to the Gentiles also the repentance {that leads} to life.**"*
(Acts 11:18)

*And the Lord's bond-servant must not be quarrelsome, but be kind to all, able to teach, patient when wronged, with gentleness correcting those who are in opposition, **if perhaps God may grant them repentance leading to the knowledge of the truth,** and they may come to their senses {and escape} from the snare of the devil, having been held captive by him to do his will.*
(2 Timothy 2:24–26)

Even after the Holy Spirit has rebuked you, it is still possible for you to refuse to repent. For example, if you stubbornly want to see your sins as something that are not all that bad, as something desirable, as something you want to continue, not as something you want to avoid, then you are not ready to repent. How could you possibly apologize for your sins under those circumstances? Your apology would be a mere formality. It would gain you nothing with God. He will only honor an apology from someone who has no intention of ever going back into sin. However, a lot of folks will never be forgiven just because they refuse to see themselves as God sees them. They are like the Pharisee that Jesus described:

> *And He also told this parable to certain ones who trusted in themselves that they were righteous, and viewed others with contempt: "Two men went up into the temple to pray, one a Pharisee, and the other a tax-gatherer. The Pharisee stood and was praying thus to himself, 'God, I thank Thee that I am not like other people: swindlers, unjust, adulterers, or even like this tax-gatherer. I fast twice a week; I pay tithes of all that I get.' But the tax-gatherer, standing some distance away, was even unwilling to lift up his eyes to heaven, but was beating his breast, saying, 'God, be merciful to me, the sinner!' I tell you, this man went down to his house justified rather than the other; **for everyone who exalts himself shall be humbled, but he who humbles himself shall be exalted."***
> *(Luke 18:9–14)*

The rebuke of the Holy Spirit plays an absolutely essential role in your salvation. That is because, without an appropriate understanding of how God views your sin, you cannot make a heartfelt apology. Therefore, if you do not agree with the rebuke of the Holy Spirit because you want to hold on to your own assessment of yourself, you cannot be forgiven. Jesus Christ died to save sinners. He did not die to save those who already see themselves as good, honest people. At least that is what He told the self-righteous Pharisees:

> *And it happened that as He was reclining {at the table} in the house, behold many tax-gatherers and sinners came and were dining with Jesus and His disciples. And when the Pharisees saw {this,} they said to His disciples, "Why is your Teacher eating with the tax-gatherers and sinners?" But when He heard this, He said, "{It is} not those who are healthy who need a physician, but those who are sick. But go and learn what {this} means, 'I DESIRE COMPASSION, AND NOT SACRIFICE,' for **I did not come to call the righteous, but sinners."***
> *(Matthew 9:10–13)*

When the Holy Spirit rebukes you, you must admit who you actually are—an incredibly sinful individual who, because of your unbelief, is capable of all sorts of depravity. That is the person you are, as opposed to the person you want to believe you are. Provided you agree with the Holy Spirit when He rebukes you, obtaining God's forgiveness is merely a matter of apologizing and asking for forgiveness. You will know He has forgiven you because the heavy weight of conviction will be lifted immediately and leave you feeling completely free from guilt. In that regard, what the Apostle John said to Believers is essentially just as true for those who are seeking salvation:

> *If we confess our sins, He is faithful and righteous to forgive us our sins and to cleanse us from all unrighteousness.*
> *(1 John 1:9)*

Well, folks, that's all there is to repentance and forgiveness of sins. All you have to do is come under the conviction of the Holy Spirit, understand and agree that your great sin is unbelief, confess your sins, accept God's forgiveness, and get on with your life. A whole lot of people have done that, and a whole lot of people have felt the tremendous emotional relief that came when the conviction of the Holy Spirit lifted after they confessed their sins and accepted God's forgiveness. Consequently, they are convinced they have been born again. They are wrong. Repentance and forgiveness of sins are essential to the new-birth process, but they are not the same as being born again. The new birth is not an emotional experience in which you ask for and *receive* God's forgiveness, it is a complete makeover of the person you have been. It is a phenomenal transformation of your perspective on this life, a renewal of your wants and desires, and a complete reordering of your value system.

To be born again you must first repent and be forgiven. But you must also hear and believe a bit more of the Gospel message than the simple Truth that God will forgive you if you ask Him. The secret to obtaining the new birth is this: You have to go to God knowing exactly what you are seeking and not stop asking until you *receive* it. Therefore, I want to explain to you what you must ask for and what God will require of you before He will grant your request.

What Is the New Birth?

Jesus said, "Repent and believe in the Gospel." I've already explained the repentance part. That is the unpleasant side of the salvation experience. Provided you know what God requires for you to be born again, the best part can come immediately after you agree with God's view of your sinful condition, apologize, and ask His forgiveness.

In the amazing wisdom of God, the new birth is exactly what the new birth requires. It is *belief* in the Gospel. It is nothing more than Jesus Christ, the Word of God, coming to life within you. That is why Jesus said the only way you will ever "see" or "enter" the *Kingdom of God*[25] is by being born again. Anyone who repents and accepts the Truth concerning Jesus Christ has that Truth living within them. But the only way the Word can do that is

---

[25] John 3:3, 5.

if you accept the one essential Truth that Jesus Christ is. Therefore, I am going to explain the single most important Truth you must accept concerning Jesus Christ, the *Living* Word of God. Along "*The Way*" however, I am going to sketch a bare-bones outline of God's eternal plan of salvation. First, take a look at how Jesus explained the new birth to Nicodemus:

> *Now there was a man of the Pharisees, named Nicodemus, a ruler of the Jews; this man came to Him by night, and said to Him, "Rabbi, we know that You have come from God {as} a teacher; for no one can do these signs that You do unless God is with him." Jesus answered and said to him,* **"Truly, truly, I say to you, unless one is born again, he cannot see the kingdom of God."** *Nicodemus said to Him, "How can a man be born when he is old? He cannot enter a second time into his mother's womb and be born, can he?" Jesus answered,* **"Truly, truly, I say to you, unless one is born of water and the Spirit, he cannot enter into the kingdom of God. That which is born of the flesh is flesh, and that which is born of the Spirit is spirit. Do not marvel that I said to you, 'You must be born again.' The wind blows where it wishes and you hear the sound of it, but do not know where it comes from and where it is going; so is everyone who is born of the Spirit."** *Nicodemus answered and said to Him, "How can these things be?" Jesus answered and said to him, "Are you the teacher of Israel, and do not understand these things? Truly, truly, I say to you, we speak that which we know, and bear witness of that which we have seen; and you do not receive our witness. If I told you earthly things and you do not believe, how shall you believe if I tell you heavenly things? And no one has ascended into heaven, but He who descended from heaven, {even} the Son of Man. And as Moses lifted up the serpent in the wilderness, even so must the Son of Man be lifted up; that whoever believes may in Him have eternal life. For God so loved the world, that He gave His only begotten Son, that whoever believes in Him should not perish, but have eternal life. For God did not send the Son into the world to judge the world, but that the world should be saved through Him. He who believes in Him is not judged; he who does not believe has been judged already, because he has not believed in the name of the only begotten Son of God.* **And this is the judgment, that the light is come into the world, and men loved the darkness rather than the light; for their deeds were evil. For everyone who does evil hates the light, and does not come to the light, lest his deeds should be exposed. But he who practices the truth comes to the light, that his deeds may be manifested as having been wrought in God."***
> (John 3:1–21)

In that passage, Jesus is describing the new-birth process, which ushers in an incredible reality that words cannot adequately explain. Therefore, I will have to explain it in the same *parabolic imagery* that Jesus used. However, to understand what Jesus said, you must first understand what John told you at the beginning of his Gospel:

> *In the beginning was the Word, and the Word was with God, and the Word was God. He was in the beginning with God. All things came into being by Him, and apart from Him nothing came into being that has come into being. In Him was life, and the life was the light of men. And the light shines in the darkness, and the darkness did not comprehend it. There came a man, sent from God, whose name was John. He came for a witness, that he might bear witness of the light, that all might believe through him. He was not the light, but {came} that he might bear witness of the light. There was the true light which, coming into the world, enlightens every man. He was in the world, and the world was made through Him, and the world did not know Him. He came to His own, and those who were His own did not receive Him. But as many as received Him, to them He gave the right to become children of God, {even} to those who believe in His name, who were born not of blood, nor of the will of the flesh, nor of the will of man, but of God.*
> (John 1:1–13)

Let me explain the *parabolic imagery* of the Prophets that John has used. "Light" *parabolically* represents Truth. Jesus Christ is the "Light" of the Word of God as opposed to the "darkness" of Satan's lies. A part of that "Light" is the Gospel message of salvation by *faith*. The "Light" of the Gospel is the same Truth that Jesus Christ is—that is, it is what He believes. If you understand that *parabolic imagery*, John's words speak for themselves. He began by telling you that Jesus Christ is "the Word of God"—that is, the Gospel—which was with God in the beginning. Only by believing that same Truth will you ever have "life." But Jesus told you that Himself elsewhere:

> *Again therefore Jesus spoke to them, saying, "I am the light of the world; he who follows Me shall not walk in the darkness, but shall have the light of life."*
> (John 8:12)

John goes on in the introduction to his Gospel to tell us, "In Him was life, and the life was the light of men." He is *talking about* the new birth ("life") that occurs when one accepts the Truth of the Gospel that Jesus Christ is. They come to life because they "see" the "Light" of the Gospel. There is no other way to be born again. That is what Jesus was *talking about* when He said this:

> *"I am the way, and the truth, and the life; no one comes to the Father, but through Me."*
> (John 14:6b)

John then says Jesus is "the true light which, coming into the world, enlightens every man." He is speaking *parabolically* concerning the Gospel as a part of *The Word of Truth* that Jesus Christ is. That Truth has the power to "enlighten" people who are living in total "darkness" (ignorance) and give them "life." However, that Truth was preached to the Jews in the time of Jesus and they rejected it. Yet John has told us that anyone who accepts the Truth of the Gospel can and will be born again:

> He came to His own, and those who were His own did not receive Him. But as many as received Him, to them He gave the right to become children of God, {even} to those who believe in His name, who were born not of blood, nor of the will of the flesh, nor of the will of man, but of God.
> (John 1:11–13)

That is a rather cursory overview of the *parabolic imagery* that explains the new-birth process. Behind that *parabolic imagery* stands an entire message in the Hebrew Scriptures concerning "Light" and its life-giving function in the plan of God. However, that message is not part of the Gospel. It is part of *The Teaching*. That Truth is not for unbelievers; it is for Believers. You must first "see" the "Light" of "the Gospel" before you can "walk" in the "Light" of *The Teaching*.

The New Covenant

The problem facing all Christian theologians today, whether they will admit it or not, is how ***the promise*** of salvation that the Apostle Paul plainly says God made to Abraham[26] suddenly became available to Gentiles. Most theologians ignore the problem, insisting that some nebulous "dispensation" or "covenant" relationship exists between the Old and New Testaments. Unfortunately for those who want to go on believing Satan's lies, there is only one explanation that adequately accounts for all the evidence of the Scriptures. You can find that explanation carefully documented in the book *Not All Israel Is Israel.*[27]

The point of that book is simple. Jesus Christ is Israel, the Firstborn Son of God. He took on that identity when He became the sole surviving member of Israel after John the Baptist, as God's appointed representative, made a New Covenant with Israel at the Jordan River. Under the terms of that New Covenant, each individual member of Israel was responsible for adhering to all the terms of the Mosaic Covenant. Anyone who failed to keep the Ten Commandments that provided the basis of the New Covenant would suffer the curse of that Law. Jesus Christ alone was able to adhere to those terms; all other Jews were "cut off from" Israel.

---

[26] Galatians 3:8.

[27] Available only through *The Voice of Elijah* (www.voiceofelijah.org).

As the sole remaining member of Israel, Jesus Christ was in complete possession of *the Promise of God*. He was God's Firstborn, *the Heir of the Promise*. Under the terms of the New Covenant He made with God, however, He would *inherit what was promised* only after He died, and only then if He remained completely obedient to God while He was alive. He did just that, therefore God responded by bringing Him back to life. That was because only then could He actually *inherit what was promised*.

That is a short synopsis of the life and death of Jesus Christ, including the reason why He was resurrected. Now comes the Truth concerning how you and I can become children of God and thus, as Paul said, "fellow heirs with Christ," heirs of *the Promise of God* with the absolutely incredible opportunity to go on to *inherit what was promised*:

> *For you have not received a spirit of slavery leading to fear again, but you have received a spirit of adoption as sons by which we cry out, "Abba! Father!" The Spirit Himself bears witness with our spirit that we are children of God, **and if children, heirs also, heirs of God and fellow heirs with Christ,** if indeed we suffer with {Him} in order that we may also be glorified with {Him.}*
> *(Romans 8:15–17)*

Having given you that little bit of information by way of background, I now want to show you the *parabolic imagery* that explains the simple Truth concerning salvation by *faith*. It can be found in the Passion narrative:

> *And on the first day of Unleavened Bread, when the Passover {lamb} was being sacrificed, His disciples said to Him, "Where do You want us to go and prepare for You to eat the Passover?" And He sent two of His disciples, and said to them, "Go into the city, and a man will meet you carrying a pitcher of water; follow him; and wherever he enters, say to the owner of the house, 'The Teacher says, "Where is My guest room in which I may eat the Passover with My disciples?"' And he himself will show you a large upper room furnished {and} ready; and prepare for us there." And the disciples went out, and came to the city, and found {it} just as He had told them; and they prepared the Passover. And when it was evening He came with the twelve. And as they were reclining {at the table} and eating, Jesus said, "Truly I say to you that one of you will betray Me—one who is eating with Me." They began to be grieved and to say to Him one by one, "Surely not I?" And He said to them, "{It is} one of the twelve, one who dips with Me in the bowl. For the Son of Man {is to} go, just as it is written of Him; but woe to that man by whom the Son of Man is betrayed! {It would have been} good for that man if he had not been born." **And while they were eating, He took {some} bread, and after a blessing He broke {it}; and gave {it} to them, and said, "Take {it}; this is My body." And when He had taken a cup, {and} given thanks, He gave {it} to them; and they all drank from it. And He said to them, "This is My blood of the covenant, which is poured out for many. Truly I say to you, I shall***

never again drink of the fruit of the vine until that day when I drink it new in the kingdom of God."
(Mark 14:12–25)

With that rather enigmatic *parabolic pantomime* involving the bread and wine, Jesus Christ and His disciples vividly depicted the Truth concerning the new-birth experience. The first key to understanding the pantomime lies in the fact that Jesus Christ is not only Israel, He is also the Truth of the Word of God. A part of that Truth is the Gospel—that is, the Truth you must accept in order to be born again.

The other key to accurately understanding the *parabolic pantomime* of eating the bread and drinking the wine resides in the fact that the purpose of a covenant meal in the Old Testament was to make everyone who participated "one people." I'll explain more about that later.

Before you can understand the statement Jesus made in the *parabolic pantomime*, I must first explain the *parabolic significance* of the bread and wine. I remind you, first of all, that the purpose of a parable (or *parabolic pantomime*) is to tell you how one thing is like another. Knowing that, it is obvious Jesus has already told us eating the bread and drinking the wine are like eating His flesh and drinking His blood. So the pantomime somehow says His death on the cross was like He was sacrificed as the Passover Lamb that provided the Passover meal at which He ratified the New Covenant He made with His disciples.

The Truth of the *parabolic pantomime* can only be seen when you remember the original Passover was itself a *parabolic pantomime* that pointed to the death of Jesus Christ as the Passover Lamb of God.[28] However, Jesus' statement concerning the bread and wine as His body and blood indicates the crucifixion itself was a *parabolic pantomime*. Therefore, the *parabolic pantomime* Jesus conducted with His disciples at the Last Supper must point to something beyond His death as the Passover Lamb of God. Otherwise, we would be left going around in a vicious circle where one pantomime refers to the other.

The insight we need lies in knowing that the Hebrews to whom God gave the Passover ritual were animistic, that is, they believed in sanctity of the soul of every living thing. Therefore, for His Own purpose, God retained that belief as a part of *The Teaching of Moses*. The following passage makes that clear. As you read, keep in mind that the Hebrew word for "soul" has been translated "life":

*"And any man from the house of Israel, or from the aliens who sojourn among them, who eats any blood, I will set My face against that person who eats blood, and will cut him off from among his people. **For the life of the flesh is in the***

---

[28] See *The Passover Parable*.

blood, and I have given it to you on the altar to make atonement for your souls; **for it is the blood by reason of the life that makes atonement.**"
(*Leviticus 17:10–11*)

God prohibited the Israelites from consuming the blood of any sacrifice because He said the "life" (soul) of the animal was in the blood. The Passover sacrifice was included under that prohibition. Therefore, only the bread that Jesus ate with His disciples can in any way point to His death as the Passover Lamb. The wine He gave them to drink points to something far, far greater. In telling His disciples they must also drink His blood, Jesus has said they must not only "consume" the "flesh" of the Person Who was sacrificed on the cross as the Passover Lamb, they must also "consume" His "life" (soul) as well. They must "consume" the very Person that He is.

The *meaning* of the *parabolic pantomime* becomes obvious only when you remember that Jesus Christ is the Word of God. He is the Truth of *The Apostolic Teaching* that He believed. Therefore, the wine in the *parabolic pantomime* points to the "wine" of the Truth that explains why Jesus Christ died on the cross as a Passover sacrifice. However, the only part of that Truth that can be "consumed"—that is, accepted and believed—by an unbeliever is the Gospel. You must believe that Truth to be born again. That is why Jesus warned His disciples that anyone who refuses to "eat" His "flesh" and "drink" His "blood" can never have the "life" provided by the new birth:

Jesus therefore said to them, "Truly, truly, I say to you, unless you eat the flesh of the Son of Man and drink His blood, you have no life in yourselves. He who eats My flesh and drinks My blood has eternal life, and I will raise him up on the last day. For My flesh is true food, and My blood is true drink. ***He who eats My flesh and drinks My blood abides in Me, and I in him.*** *As the living Father sent Me, and I live because of the Father, so he who eats Me, he also shall live because of Me. This is the bread which came down out of heaven; not as the fathers ate, and died, he who eats this bread shall live forever."*
(*John 6:53–58*)

Did you see what He said about "in Me, and I in him." He was referring to the *parabolic imagery* in which He is Israel and Believers are the "members" of His "Body." With that in mind, let me explain the *parabolic statement* Jesus made by eating bread and drinking wine with His disciples. The original Passover in Egypt was a covenant meal in which the Israelites ratified the Mosaic Covenant and thereby became "one people" in a covenant relationship with God. I have already explained that in *Not All Israel Is Israel*. According to the original *parabolic image, Corporate* Israel became God's Firstborn Son at that first Passover in Egypt. Using that same *parabolic imagery,* Jesus ate the bread and wine with His disciples to signify they were "one people" with Him under the terms of the New Covenant.

By eating the bread and drinking the wine, Jesus stated *parabolically* that the New Covenant relationship was like the disciples became His "members"— that is, "members" of the "new" or "true" Israel, however you want to look at it—by believing the Truth of the Gospel. As the Apostle Paul liked to put it, those who believe the Gospel are *"The Many,"*[29] Jesus Himself is *"The One"*:

> But the free gift is not like the transgression. For if by the transgression of **the one the many** died, much more did the grace of God and the gift by the grace of **the one** Man, Jesus Christ, abound to **the many**.
> (Romans 5:15)

> For just as we have **many members** in **one body** and all **the members** do not have the same function, so we, who are **many**, are **one body** in Christ, and individually **members** one of another.
> (Romans 12:4–5)

> Since there is **one bread**, we who are **many** are **one body**; for we all partake of **the one bread**.
> (1 Corinthians 10:17)

The "one people" relationship Jesus *parabolically* established with His disciples is the most significant aspect of the New Covenant. By the simple act of uniting Himself with these men through their **belief** in Him, Jesus Christ became guilty of their sins. Under the terms of His Own New Covenant relationship with God, the sins of His "members" demanded that He die as a sacrifice for their sins because their sins were now His Own. As the Apostle Peter said:

> And He Himself bore our sins in His body on the cross, that we might die to sin and live to righteousness; for by His wounds you were healed.
> (1 Peter 2:24)

Under the circumstances I have just described for you, the Apostle Peter had good reason to say that Jesus Christ "bore our sins." He was one of the disciples who participated directly in the *parabolic pantomime*. He ate the *parabolic* bread and drank the *parabolic* wine with Jesus. But the fact that eleven Jewish fellows *parabolically* entered into a covenant relationship with Jesus Christ (Judas Iscariot didn't believe) doesn't explain why Paul could say this:

> **Christ redeemed us from the curse of the Law, having become a curse for us**—for it is written, "CURSED IS EVERYONE WHO HANGS ON A TREE"—**in order that in Christ Jesus the blessing of Abraham might come to the Gentiles, so that we might receive the promise of the Spirit through faith.**
> (Galatians 3:13–14)

---

[29] Daniel 12:3.

Paul is not *talking about* just the eleven disciples who *parabolically* ratified a covenant with Jesus Christ at the Lord's Supper. He has included Gentiles as well. How could that be? Well, the Apostle John has given us the one passage of Scripture that concisely explains how others, Gentiles as well as Jews, came to be included under the terms of the New Covenant.

In the following prayer in the Garden, Jesus asks His Father to include "those also who believe in Me through their word; that they may all be one; even as Thou, Father, {art} in Me, and I in Thee, that they also may be in Us." As you read the words of Jesus, keep in mind that the bread and wine *parabolically* represent Jesus Christ as "the Word" of the Gospel. Then notice that, in His prayer, Jesus *talks about* the fact that He has given that "Word" to His disciples so that they could become "one" with Him. That merely emphasizes the fact that the bread and the wine were *parabolic* symbols. Belief in "the Word" of the Gospel is all that Jesus Christ has ever required of anyone who desires to participate in the New Covenant relationship with Him:

> *"I manifested Thy name to the men whom Thou gavest Me out of the world; Thine they were, and Thou gavest them to Me, and they have kept Thy word.* **Now they have come to know that everything Thou hast given Me is from Thee; for the words which Thou gavest Me I have given to them; and they received {them,} and truly understood that I came forth from Thee, and they believed that Thou didst send Me. I ask on their behalf; I do not ask on behalf of the world, but of those whom Thou hast given Me; for they are Thine; and all things that are Mine are Thine, and Thine are Mine; and I have been glorified in them.** *And I am no more in the world; and {yet} they themselves are in the world, and I come to Thee. Holy Father, keep them in Thy name, {the name} which Thou hast given Me, that they may be one, even as We {are}. While I was with them, I was keeping them in Thy name which Thou hast given Me; and I guarded them, and not one of them perished but the son of perdition, that the Scripture might be fulfilled. But now I come to Thee; and these things I speak in the world, that they may have My joy made full in themselves.* **I have given them Thy word; and the world has hated them, because they are not of the world, even as I am not of the world.** *I do not ask Thee to take them out of the world, but to keep them from the evil {one.} They are not of the world, even as I am not of the world.* **Sanctify them in the truth; Thy word is truth.** *As Thou didst send Me into the world, I also have sent them into the world. And for their sakes I sanctify Myself, that they themselves also may be sanctified in truth.* **I do not ask in behalf of these alone, but for those also who believe in Me through their word; that they may all be one; even as Thou, Father, {art} in Me, and I in Thee, that they also may be in Us; that the world may believe that Thou didst send Me. And the glory which Thou hast given Me I have given to them; that they may be one, just as We are one; I in them, and Thou in Me,**

that they may be perfected in unity, that the world may know that Thou didst send Me, and didst love them, even as Thou didst love Me. Father, I desire that they also, whom Thou hast given Me, be with Me where I am, in order that they may behold My glory, which Thou hast given Me; for Thou didst love Me before the foundation of the world."
(John 17:6–24)

That prayer expresses the essence of what Jesus stated by eating the bread and drinking the wine with His disciples. He *parabolically* ratified a New Covenant with them so that all who believe the Truth of the Gospel might become "one" with Him in God; or, according to the *parabolic image* the Apostle Paul was so fond of using, they might become "members" of His "Body":

*And by referring to this, when you read you can understand my insight into the mystery of Christ, which in other generations was not made known to the sons of men, as it has now been revealed to His holy apostles and prophets in the Spirit; {to be specific}, **that the Gentiles are fellow heirs and fellow members of the body, and fellow partakers of the promise in Christ Jesus through the gospel,** of which I was made a minister, according to the gift of God's grace which was given to me according to the working of His power.*
(Ephesians 3:4–7)

That explains how Jesus Christ accomplished salvation for all those who would ever believe the Gospel down through the ages. Through the agency of the New Covenant, He took upon Himself the sins of all who have ever or will ever **believe**, and He died as the Passover sacrifice that they must "consume" in order to become "one" with Him.

The *parabolic statement* Jesus made in which the bread and wine represent His flesh and blood merely tells us we must **believe** The Word of Truth concerning His death and Resurrection. In other words, if we **believe** the Gospel, we will become a member of the Body of Jesus Christ. And, "in Christ" we become "one" with Christ and take on the "life" of Christ Himself, thereby becoming a new person, just as the Apostle Paul said:

*Therefore **if any man is in Christ,** {he is} **a new creature;** the old things passed away; behold, new things have come.*
(2 Corinthians 5:17)

The new birth occurs when a True Believer "consumes" the Truth of the Gospel so that he/she becomes "one" with that Truth. According to the *parabolic imagery* used, the Truth of "the Word" that Jesus Christ is becomes a "new" or "inner" person within the True Believer. Paul *talks about* that astounding transformation in various places.[30] Amazingly, in some way that

---

[30] Romans 7:22; 2 Corinthians 4:16; 5:17; Ephesians 2:15; 3:16.

I cannot adequately explain (because it is also a *parabolic statement*) the Truth they have believed is now the new person that they are! That new birth is nothing less than a gift from God. You can do nothing to deserve it. It is the gift of God/the Holy Spirit that you find mentioned throughout the Scriptures:

> *Jesus answered and said to her, "If you knew* **the gift of God,** *and who it is who says to you, 'Give Me a drink,' you would have asked Him, and He would have given you living water."*
> *(John 4:10)*

> *And Peter {said} to them,* **"Repent, and let each of you be baptized in the name of Jesus Christ for the forgiveness of your sins; and you shall receive the gift of the Holy Spirit."**
> *(Acts 2:38)*

> *But Peter said to him, "May your silver perish with you, because you thought you could obtain* **the gift of God** *with money!"*
> *(Acts 8:20)*

> *And all the circumcised believers who had come with Peter were amazed, because* **the gift of the Holy Spirit** *had been poured out upon the Gentiles also.*
> *(Acts 10:45)*

> *For the wages of sin is death, but* **the free gift of God** *is eternal life in Christ Jesus our Lord.*
> *(Romans 6:23)*

> *For by grace you have been saved through faith; and that not of yourselves, {it is}* **the gift of God.**
> *(Ephesians 2:8)*

> *And for this reason I remind you to kindle afresh* **the gift of God** *which is in you through the laying on of my hands.*
> *(2 Timothy 1:6)*

> *"If you then, being evil, know how to* **give good gifts** *to your children, how much more shall {your} heavenly Father* **give the Holy Spirit** *to those who ask Him?"*
> *(Luke 11:13)*

The new birth is freely given to all who *believe* the Gospel. That gift of God/the Holy Spirit is yours because, in *believing* the Gospel, you have joined yourself to Jesus Christ and have made His nature your own. As a member of His "Body," you no longer stand under the judgment of God because Christ has already endured the penalty of sin for you. Consequently, you are now "justified as a gift":

*But now apart from the Law {the} righteousness of God has been manifested, being witnessed by the Law and the Prophets, even {the} righteousness of God through faith in Jesus Christ for all those who believe; for there is no distinction; for all have sinned and fall short of the glory of God, **being justified as a gift by His grace through the redemption which is in Christ Jesus;** whom God displayed publicly as a propitiation in His blood through faith. {This was} to demonstrate His righteousness, because in the forbearance of God He passed over the sins previously committed; for the demonstration, {I say,} of His righteousness at the present time, that He might be just and the justifier of the one who has faith in Jesus.* (Romans 3:21–26)

Paul *talks about* that same thing in other places as well. The secret to understanding what he has said always lies in the fact that, by becoming "one" with Jesus Christ, you have transferred your sins to Him and have taken on His righteousness and holiness:

*Nevertheless death reigned from Adam until Moses, even over those who had not sinned in the likeness of the offense of Adam, who is a type of Him who was to come. **But the free gift is not like the transgression. For if by the transgression of the one the many died, much more did the grace of God and the gift by the grace of the one Man, Jesus Christ, abound to the many. And the gift is not like {that which came} through the one who sinned;** for on the one hand the judgment {arose} from one {transgression} resulting in condemnation, but on the other hand **the free gift {arose} from many transgressions resulting in justification.** For if by the transgression of the one, death reigned through the one, much more those who receive the abundance of grace and of the gift of righteousness will reign in life through the One, Jesus Christ. So then as through one transgression there resulted condemnation to all men, even so through one act of righteousness there resulted justification of life to all men. For as through the one man's disobedience the many were made sinners, even so **through the obedience of the One the many will be made righteous.*** (Romans 5:14–19)

That's all there is to it, folks! Jesus Christ did it all for you. All you have to do is *believe*.

How Dumb Can You Be?

I could explain other benefits that derive from the mystical union with Jesus Christ, but those things are a part of *The Teaching*, and as such are reserved for True Believers. I have mentioned only a few of the things here that allow you to understand the phenomenal gift that God offers everyone, and freely gives to anyone who believes the Truth of the Gospel. The gift of the Holy Spirit completes your union with God the Father through Jesus

Christ the Son. You are *"in* Christ" when you believe the Truth. Christ is *"in* you" when you accept the gift of God/the Holy Spirit. That is nothing more than *parabolic imagery* that explains an awesome supernatural reality. It does not tell you WHAT THAT REALITY IS, it only tells you WHAT THAT REALITY IS LIKE. However, Paul uses the same *parabolic imagery* in the following passages to *talk about* the things I have already explained:

> *In Him, you also, after listening to the message of truth, the gospel of your salvation—having also believed, you were sealed in Him with the Holy Spirit of promise,* who is given as a pledge of our inheritance, with a view to the redemption of {God's own} possession, to the praise of His glory.
> (Ephesians 1:13–14)

> Of {this church} I was made a minister according to the stewardship from God bestowed on me for your benefit, that I might fully carry out the {preaching of} the word of God, {that is,} the mystery which has been hidden from the {past} ages and generations; but has now been manifested to His saints, to whom God willed to make known what is **the riches of the glory of this mystery among the Gentiles, which is Christ in you, the hope of glory.**
> (Colossians 1:25–27)

I have now come to the fly in the ointment as far as some are concerned. You see, only an incredibly stupid individual would pass up God's offer of eternal life, especially when it is freely given and all you have to do is **believe.** Notice I said "it is freely given." I did not say "it costs you nothing." That is because God's free gift costs you everything you ever have been. As the Apostle Paul wrote to the Galatians, a person must die before Christ can live within them:

> *"I have been crucified with Christ; and it is no longer I who live, but Christ lives in me; and the {life} which I now live in the flesh I live by faith in the Son of God, who loved me, and delivered Himself up for me."*
> (Galatians 2:20)

Paul is merely using the *parabolic imagery* of *"in* Christ" and "Christ *in* you." That *parabolic imagery* tells you WHAT THE REALITY OF THE NEW BIRTH IS LIKE. Before you can be born again, you must willingly give up the person you have been and accept the Person God wants you to be. To see how that is, take a look at how Paul described the simplicity of the Gospel message:

> But the righteousness based on faith speaks thus, "DO NOT SAY IN YOUR HEART, 'WHO WILL ASCEND INTO HEAVEN?' (that is, to bring Christ down), or 'WHO WILL DESCEND INTO THE ABYSS?' (that is, to bring Christ up from the dead)." But what does it say? "THE WORD IS NEAR YOU, IN YOUR MOUTH AND IN YOUR HEART"—that is, the word of faith which we are preaching, that **if you confess with your mouth Jesus {as} Lord, and believe in your heart that God raised**

Him from the dead, you shall be saved; for with the heart man believes, resulting in righteousness, and with the mouth he confesses, resulting in salvation.
(Romans 10:6–10)

That passage has just told you that, to accept the free gift God has to offer, you must "confess with your mouth Jesus as Lord." That's too big a step for some folks. They will confess their sins and ask forgiveness, but they like their independence too much to confess Jesus Christ as "Lord." So they turn away from God with only the emotional experience of having been forgiven and they spend the rest of their lives as Pretenders in the Church.

What does Paul *mean* when he says "confess with your mouth Jesus as Lord"? Well, it's one of those "you can pay me now, or you can pay me later" kind of things. To understand what he *means*, take a look at the following passage:

*Have this attitude in yourselves which was also in Christ Jesus, who, although He existed in the form of God, did not regard equality with God a thing to be grasped, but emptied Himself, taking the form of a bond-servant, {and} being made in the likeness of men. And being found in appearance as a man, He humbled Himself by becoming obedient to the point of death, even death on a cross. **Therefore also God highly exalted Him, and bestowed on Him the name which is above every name, that at the name of Jesus EVERY KNEE SHOULD BOW, of those who are in heaven, and on earth, and under the earth, and that every tongue should confess that Jesus Christ is Lord, to the glory of God the Father.***
(Philippians 2:5–11)

Did you see that? Everybody is going to "confess that Jesus Christ is Lord" before going off to their eternal destiny. However, the key to your salvation lies in the fact that, after **hearing** and **believing** the Truth of the Gospel, you will be able to accept the fact that Jesus Christ is "Lord" before you stand before Him at the Judgment. Therefore, you can "confess" that fact now, rather than waiting until it is too late.

What does it actually *mean* to "confess with your mouth Jesus as Lord"? The answer lies in the fact that "at the name of Jesus every knee should bow." It *means* you "confess" Jesus Christ alone has the "right" to reign as King over you and you submit to His authority. "Lord" is the throne "name" that God gave to Jesus Christ because of His obedience in keeping the terms of the New Covenant. It reflects His "right" to reign as King over all. That fact has already been demonstrated by His Resurrection, which is why Paul said that, "if you confess with your mouth Jesus {as} Lord, and believe in your heart that God raised Him from the dead, you shall be saved."

But to whom do you "confess" Jesus Christ as Lord? To anyone who will listen, but especially to Jesus Christ Himself when you ask for the gift of His

Holy Spirit. Why so? Because the only way you will ever be born again—that is, the only way you will ever gain entry into His Kingdom, which is the "Kingdom of Heaven/God/Light"—is to swear obedience to Him alone. You must do that verbally, "with your mouth." If you do not submit voluntarily to the King of Kings down here, you will have no part "in Him." That is because, contrary to what Satan would have you believe, Jesus Christ is the only "Lord" there is:

For even if there are so-called gods whether in heaven or on earth, as indeed there are many gods and many lords, yet for us there is {but} one God, the Father, from whom are all things, and we {exist} for Him; and one Lord, Jesus Christ, by whom are all things, and we {exist} through Him.
(1 Corinthians 8:5–6)

You can get some idea of the *significance* of the term *Lord* from what Paul says in the following passage where, because the translator didn't understand Paul's point concerning the "name" that Jesus Christ has been given, the term has been translated both "Lord" and "master":

*Slaves, be obedient to those who are your **masters** according to the flesh, with fear and trembling, in the sincerity of your heart, as to Christ; not by way of eyeservice, as men-pleasers, but as slaves of Christ, doing the will of God from the heart. With good will render service, as to **the Lord**, and not to men, knowing that whatever good thing each one does, this he will receive back from **the Lord**, whether slave or free. And, **masters**, do the same things to them, and give up threatening, knowing that both their **Master** and yours is in heaven, and there is no partiality with Him. Finally, be strong in **the Lord**, and in the strength of His might.*
(Ephesians 6:5–10)

The point is, Jesus Christ has every "right" to demand your absolute obedience—an obedience equal to that of a slave—because of what He has done for you. If you are not willing to make that commitment, you cannot, and will not, be born again. I don't care what anybody tells you about "praying the sinner's prayer" and "confessing" your salvation to others, the only essential "confession" you must make is to Jesus Christ Himself. If you do not swear perfect obedience to Him alone and promise Him your unquestioning loyalty, the only thing your "confession" will gain you is the following:

*"**Not everyone who says to Me, 'Lord, Lord,' will enter the kingdom of heaven; but he who does the will of My Father who is in heaven. Many will say to Me on that day, 'Lord, Lord,** did we not prophesy in Your name, and in Your name cast out demons, and in Your name perform many miracles?' And then I will declare to them, 'I never knew you; DEPART FROM ME, YOU WHO PRACTICE LAWLESSNESS.'"*
(Matthew 7:21–23)

A Bit About Lies and Liars

What do you think? Have you ever made the commitment God requires for you to be born again? If you have any doubt at all, I suggest you err on the side of safety and start seeking the Lord's salvation. DON'T EVER ASK FOR CONFIRMATION THAT YOU HAVE BEEN BORN AGAIN. If you haven't been born again and merely ask for assurance that you have been, you will never be born again because you have not asked. Ask first that the Holy Spirit "rebuke" you. When He does that, ask God's forgiveness, accept the Lordship of Christ, and ask for the gift of the Holy Spirit. If you have already been born again and do that, I have no doubt God will, in His mercy, provide you all the assurance you need.

In regard to the "assurance of salvation," let me mention a couple of lies that Satan has sown in the Church for the specific purpose of deluding those who desire to be saved. The foremost lie of Satan goes something like this: "Everybody's new-birth experience is different because it's all by faith, not by feelings." To a certain extent, that's true. Everybody responds to the Lord in their own particular way, and salvation certainly is by *faith* (belief), not by feelings. But there are some things about the new-birth experience that are exactly the same for everyone, so let me list them for you: (1) feeling the "rebuke" or "conviction" of the Holy Spirit, (2) feeling the freedom from guilt that follows your confession of sin and request for forgiveness, and (3) feeling the complete transformation that occurs when you are born again. So much for the idiots who want to tell you feelings are not a part of the new-birth experience. If you have no idea what feelings I am *talking about*, don't let the liars in the Church convince you that you have been born again. You haven't, and neither have they.

I have already mentioned the one lie of Satan that, more than any other, is going to shepherd a multitude of Pretenders into the pits of hell. That is the *belief* that the new birth is nothing more than the emotional release that occurs when a person honestly repents, God forgives, and the conviction of the Holy Spirit immediately goes away. Unless the new birth follows that emotional experience, repentance produces nothing more than a Pharisaic legalist. This type of Pretender knows he should not sin, and he tries not to sin, but he doesn't have the Holy Spirit within enabling him to overcome sin. Therefore, he resorts to a list of do's and don'ts to provide him the assurance of salvation he lacks. Some of these people are not all that far from the Kingdom of Heaven, provided they (1) hear the Truth, (2) realize their legalism has given them nothing but the pride of accomplishment, (3) respond by renouncing the lie they have believed, and (4) seek the new birth on God's terms like any other sinner. If they refuse to *believe* the Truth, God hates them all the more because they responded to the conviction of the Spirit once but now want nothing more to do with the Truth.

The final lie of Satan is the one he is pushing more vigorously than any other today. That is the "confess Jesus Christ" stupidity you hear everywhere. What can be said about total ignorance? The Pretenders who believe this lie are not responding honestly to any genuine conviction of the Holy Spirit. They are merely making an intellectual decision to "follow Christ," whatever that *means* to them. God demands much more than an intellectual decision. He seeks a total commitment of your entire being so that you can be born again. That commitment begins with the conviction, the "rebuke," of the Holy Spirit. Most of the people who respond to the ridiculous "confess Jesus" nonsense are seeking some way to hide from that conviction.

Rights and Responsibilities

If you have been born again, God has called me as a Teacher to teach you the things you need to know to prepare for the persecution that will occur during the reign of the Antichrist. I have no doubt the seven messages hidden in the Hebrew Scriptures will absolutely astound you. If you haven't been born again, I also have the "right" as an Evangelist to introduce you to "*The One*" Who is the Kingdom of "Light." I have already exercised that "right" by explaining the basics of the Gospel in this book. The rest is up to you. No salesman will call. But the Spirit of Jesus Christ will, if you ask. So when you feel His "rebuke," here's all you need to do: (1) place your hands on this book; (2) ask God to forgive you; and (3) when you feel the conviction of the Holy Spirit lift, submit completely to the Lord Jesus Christ as your "Master" and tell Him you have done so; then (4) ask for the gift of the Holy Spirit; and (5) accept it.

Now let me tell you why I told you to place your hands on this book before you ask God's forgiveness. There is nothing magical involved. It is merely a point of contact through which you *receive* the "right" to become a child of God. You have probably watched an Evangelist on television at one time or another who told viewers to place their hands on the television while he prayed. He may not know it, but the point of that exercise is for people to signify submission to his authority as an Evangelist.

I have already explained that Jesus Christ demands you submit to Him as "Lord" before you can be born again. He *received* that "right"—that is, that authority—from God Himself. I have also explained the authority that Christ gave to the Church. I told you that the men whom God called to minister in the four offices of the Church had whatever "right" was attached to their particular office. Apostles, Prophets, and Teachers have not ministered in the Church for centuries; but Evangelists have. And every legitimate Evangelist has had the "right" to give unbelievers the "right"—that is, the authority—to become children of God by preaching the Gospel to them. That's what John *meant* when he wrote this:

He came to His own, and those who were His own did not receive Him. But as
*many as received Him, to them **He gave the right to become children of God,***
{even} to those who believe in His name.
(John 1:11–12)

It was common practice in the Early Church for Church leaders to transfer authority ("right") by the laying on of hands. You can find various
instances in the Book of Acts where the Apostles transferred the "right" for
someone to become a child of God by laying hands on them. One of the
most misunderstood passages is the one where the Apostles went down to
Samaria to lay hands on the first Samaritan Believers:

Now when the apostles in Jerusalem heard that Samaria had received the word of
God, they sent them Peter and John, who came down and prayed for them, that
they might receive the Holy Spirit. For He had not yet fallen upon any of them;
they had simply been baptized in the name of the Lord Jesus. Then they {began}
laying their hands on them, and they were receiving the Holy Spirit.
(Acts 8:14–17)

The point of the passage has to do with the fact that God required the
Samaritans to submit to the authority of the Jewish Apostles before they
could be born again. My point here is that the authority to become a child of
God was routinely transferred through the laying on of hands. Paul even
mentions it in connection with Timothy's new-birth experience:

And for this reason I remind you to kindle afresh the gift of God which is in you
through the laying on of my hands.
(2 Timothy 1:6)

Apostles, Prophets, Teachers, and Evangelists laid hands on people in
the Early Church as a sign that they were transferring some "right" to
them—for example, the "right" to become a child of God, the "right" to be
"delivered" from Satan's bondage, etc. The acceptance of that ritual by others was a sign of their submission to the authority "the Lord" gave the
Church. Although I haven't discussed the transfer of authority in connection with healing and casting out demons, the principle remains the same.
The transfer of the "right" to be healed in the following passage tells us it
could be accomplished remotely by other means:

And God was performing extraordinary miracles by the hands of Paul, so that
handkerchiefs or aprons were even carried from his body to the sick, and the dis-
eases left them and the evil spirits went out.
(Acts 19:11–12)

I don't have time here to explain everything related to the laying on of
hands. As the Book of Hebrews mentions, those things are a basic part of *The*

Teaching.[31] I merely want to emphasize that Christ established the Church by giving the Apostles the authority He *received* from God the Father. That was His absolute authority as "Lord." So, by laying your hands on this book, you are signifying you understand your "right" to become a child of God is based on the fact that Jesus Christ, as "Lord" of all Creation, gave the Church the "right" to preach the Gospel so that you might be saved. That's what the new birth is all about anyway—submission to the authority of Jesus Christ. All that other stuff I explained is just *parabolic pantomime* to help you understand how God looks at your circumstances.

Postscript

While I'm on the subject of the authority Christ gave the Church, let me say a few things more. I have explained that God reacts in anger toward people who hear the Truth but don't accept it. One of the things that especially angers Him is True Believers overstepping the bounds of whatever authority they have *received*. For example, an Evangelist can do that by preaching things other than the Gospel. A Teacher can do that by teaching unbelievers. (Believe me, I know all about that from personal experience.) However, God harbors a special hatred for anybody who ministers in the Church when they have no authority at all to do so. That is because these people, in their ignorance, are nothing more than agents of Satan, teaching a mixture of Truth and lies.

If you have been teaching others the things you have learned from me, I can guarantee you the wrath of God is burning against you. I know that because I know that God has not called you as a Teacher. If He had, you would not be getting your knowledge of *The Teaching* from me. Now that I've told you how God views such activity, I have absolved myself of all responsibility for what you do with what I teach. The one thing I will do is pray that, if you do such things, the Holy Spirit Himself will rebuke you openly so that you understand what I have said. Perhaps then you will refrain from such nonsense.

While I'm on the subject of people who teach a mixture of Truth and lies, let me mention one particular mix that God finds especially offensive. You see, people have come up with some ingenious doctrinal innovations to explain what has happened to those who first experienced the freedom from guilt that follows repentance and then, at some later time, experienced the complete transformation that is the new birth. For example, the Gospel message that many heard when they repented during the First Great Awakening was not sufficient to result in their new birth. Hence, they were born again later and were convinced they had a second salvation experience.

---

[31] Hebrews 6:2.

John Wesley saw what was happening and decided there was a "second definite work of grace" called "sanctification." Therefore, you may have heard someone say they have been "saved and sanctified."

The Pentecostal revivals at the beginning of the 20th century grew out of the late 19th century revivals in the Holiness Movement. Holiness folks firmly believed there was a "second definite work of grace." So that doctrine provided the basis for Pentecostal beliefs regarding the "baptism of the Holy Spirit" as an experience subsequent to the new birth. Yet what was actually happening in the Pentecostal revivals was exactly the same as what John Wesley observed. Some people were accepting God's forgiveness at one time and receiving the gift of the Holy Spirit (the new birth) sometime later. Others were merely receiving the gift of tongues subsequent to the new birth.

Some Pentecostal leaders thought the account in the Book of Acts fit the Wesleyan pattern. Others believed the "baptism/gift of the Holy Spirit" was the last of three distinct spiritual experiences: (1) the new birth, (2) sanctification, and (3) the baptism of the Holy Spirit. Although Believers born again during those revivals had no doubt as to the reality of what they had experienced, John Wesley and the leaders of the Pentecostal movement went well beyond their authority as Evangelists when they crafted the goofiness related to a "second definite work of grace." Not only were they trying to teach Believers, which they had no authority at all to do, they were corrupting the simple message of salvation by *faith* in the process. In God's sight, that was a travesty.

In what I have just said, I am in no way denying the validity of the Pentecostal experience of speaking in tongues. As the Apostle Paul said:

> I thank God, I speak in tongues more than you all.
> (1 Corinthians 14:18)

However, there is no second or third salvation experience. There is only the freedom from guilt that follows true repentance and the phenomenal spiritual transformation brought about by the new birth, which is throughout the New Testament referred to as "the gift/baptism of the Holy Spirit." I will readily admit that many have been left thinking the feeling of freedom from guilt that they experienced when they were forgiven is the new birth. They believe that only because they have not heard enough of the Gospel to be born again, or because Pretenders have encouraged them to believe Satan's lie. Hopefully, some will be enlightened by what I say here and start seeking the free gift that God has to offer all those who have opportunity to hear and believe the Truth.

7 Simple Steps to Salvation

Repentance is nothing but an *honest* apology that comes from the heart. That *honest* apology is the key to the new birth; but the source of the apology is a sincere belief in the Truth of the Gospel. That is, before one can—or will—*honestly* apologize, he must have some good reason to apologize. The Truth of the Gospel provides an extremely good reason to apologize—provided one believes it. Jesus said this:

> But after John was handed over, Jesus came into Galilee, preaching the Gospel of the {Living} God and saying, "Since the time [has been filled completely and the kingdom] of the {Living} God has draw near, **apologize and believe in the Gospel.**"
> *(Mark 1:14–15) —my translation*

In that passage, Jesus briefly mentions the crucial link that exists between believing the Truth and *honestly* apologizing. But in this passage, He gives good reason for any reasonable person to apologize:

> But some were present at the same time who reported to Him concerning the Galileans of whom Pilate mingled the blood with the sacrifices they had. And responding, He said to them, "Are you assuming that these Galileans were sinners above all the Galileans because they suffered these {things}? **Absolutely not, I say to you, but if you do not apologize, you will all likewise be done away with.** Or those eighteen on whom the tower of Siloam fell and killed them? Are you assuming that they were obligated above all the men—the {ones} who were residing {in} Jerusalem? **Absolutely not, I say to you, but if you do not apologize, you will all similarly be done away with.**"
> *(Luke 13:1–5) —my translation*

The *honest* apology that God requires has two distinct components. The first is a change of mind that drives the person to apologize; the second is the change of direction that follows his apology. The Gospel provides all the information one needs to have the required change of mind; but the fear that sets in when one truly believes is the only way anyone can gain the required change of direction. That is, if you do the first—believe the Truth of the Gospel and *honestly* apologize—God will grant you the second.

Pretenders skip the *honest* apology because their pride, arrogance, and stubbornness will not allow them to submit to Christ. Therefore, they do the ultimate stupid thing; they pretend. They fake the change of direction that follows the new-birth experience just to fit in with True Believers. Unfortunately, they are putting a new "patch" on an old "garment." God is never going to accept anyone who does not *honestly* apologize for what they know they have done wrong; and that *honest* apology is not possible unless you actually feel sorry for sinning against God, rather than feeling sorry for yourself. That is why Paul says this:

> For the anguish in agreement with God works an apology into an unchanging sal-
> vation. But the anguish of the world brings about death.
> (2 Corinthians 7:10) —my translation

Honestly feeling sorry for your sins is not possible unless you actually believe the Truth of the Gospel. That is, you have to believe *you are not going to be judged*; you have to believe *you have already been judged*. As Jesus said:

> "For God did not send the Son into the world to judge the world, but that the world
> should be saved through Him. **He who believes in Him is not judged; he who
> does not believe has been judged already, because he has not believed in the
> name of the only begotten Son of God."**
> (John 3:17–18)

All that remains for those who refuse to apologize is sentencing to the horror of an eternity of torment with no hope of redemption. Judgment Day is not about assessing guilt, it is about assessing severity of punishment. Your only hope is to somehow gain a pardon before that Great Day. And "*The* {only} *Way*" you will ever *honestly* seek that pardon is if you *honestly* believe the Truth of the Gospel. That is because an *honest* belief in the Gospel leads to a distinct fear of what God is going to do to you if you do not apologize. So let me give a set of step-by-step instructions concerning what you must believe.

1. You must believe there is a God who will respond to you favorably if you apologize:

> And without faith it is impossible to please {Him}, for he who comes to God must
> believe that He is, and {that} He is a rewarder of those who seek Him.
> (Hebrews 11:6)

2. You must believe that you stand guilty before God. God does not save victims; He will only respond to those who take responsibility for their own actions:

If we say that we have no sin, we are deceiving ourselves, and the truth is not in us.
(1 John 1:8)

3. You must believe God is going to destroy you if you do not *honestly* apologize; but He will also reward you with eternal life if you do:

For the wages of sin is death, but the free gift of God is eternal life in Christ Jesus our Lord.
(Romans 6:23)

4. You must believe that God *fulfilled the promise* when He resurrected Jesus Christ in His Own image and likeness, and that He will also resurrect True Believers at the End of the Age:

Now if Christ is preached, that He has been raised from the dead, how do some among you say that there is no resurrection of the dead? But if there is no resurrection of the dead, not even Christ has been raised.
(1 Corinthians 15:12–13)

For if we have become united with {Him} in the likeness of His death, certainly we shall be also {in the likeness} of His resurrection.
(Romans 6:5)

5. You must believe there is absolutely nothing you can do to be worthy of *the promise* of resurrection in the image and likeness of God. That is, you must believe that comes strictly as a "favor" (translated "grace") from God on the basis of your belief in the Truth of *the promise*:

For this reason {it is} by faith, that {it might be} in accordance with grace, in order that the promise may be certain to all the descendants, not only to those who are of the Law, but also to those who are of the faith of Abraham, who is the father of us all.
(Romans 4:16)

For by grace you have been saved through faith; and that not of yourselves, {it is} the gift of God.
(Ephesians 2:8)

6. You must accept the fact that Jesus Christ has already been anointed as *the promised* King Who is going to rule in the Age to Come. He is, in fact, God Himself; and you must accept Him as your Lord and Master:

But the righteousness based on faith speaks thus, "DO NOT SAY IN YOUR HEART, 'WHO WILL ASCEND INTO HEAVEN?' (that is, to bring Christ down), or 'WHO WILL DESCEND INTO THE ABYSS?' (that is, to bring Christ up from the dead)." But what does it say? "THE WORD IS NEAR YOU, IN YOUR MOUTH AND IN YOUR HEART"—that is, the word of faith which we are preaching, that if you confess with your mouth Jesus {as} Lord, and believe in your heart that God raised Him from the dead, you shall be saved; for with the heart man believes, resulting in righteous-

ness, and with the mouth he confesses, resulting in salvation.
(Romans 10:6–10)

7. You must submit yourself to Christ with a complete willingness to do whatever you believe is the "right" thing for you to do without demanding that it must also be the "right" thing for others to do. That is, Christ has the authority to tell you what you must do, but you do not have the authority to tell others what they must do:

Therefore you are without excuse, every man {of you} who passes judgment, for in that you judge another, you condemn yourself; for you who judge practice the same things. And we know that the judgment of God rightly falls upon those who practice such things. And do you suppose this, O man, when you pass judgment upon those who practice such things and do the same {yourself,} that you will escape the judgment of God? Or do you think lightly of the riches of His kindness and forbearance and patience, not knowing that the kindness of God leads you to repentance? But because of your stubbornness and unrepentant heart you are storing up wrath for yourself in the day of wrath and revelation of the righteous judgment of God, who WILL RENDER TO EVERY MAN ACCORDING TO HIS DEEDS: to those who by perseverance in doing good seek for glory and honor and immortality, eternal life; but to those who are selfishly ambitious and do not obey the truth, but obey unrighteousness, wrath and indignation.
(Romans 2:1–8)

If you *honestly* believe the things I have explained concerning *the promise*, all you have to do to be born again is apologize. And if you take the seven simple steps to salvation I outlined above, you will be born again:

For the Scripture says, "WHOEVER BELIEVES IN HIM WILL NOT BE DISAPPOINTED." For there is no distinction between Jew and Greek; for the same {Lord} is Lord of all, abounding in riches for all who call upon Him; for "WHOEVER WILL CALL UPON THE NAME OF THE LORD WILL BE SAVED." How then shall they call upon Him in whom they have not believed? And how shall they believe in Him whom they have not heard? And how shall they hear without a preacher? And how shall they preach unless they are sent? Just as it is written, "HOW BEAUTIFUL ARE THE FEET OF THOSE WHO BRING GLAD TIDINGS OF GOOD THINGS!" However, they did not all heed the glad tidings; for Isaiah says, "LORD, WHO HAS BELIEVED OUR REPORT?" So faith {comes} from hearing, and hearing by the word of Christ. But I say, surely they have never heard, have they? Indeed they have;

"THEIR VOICE HAS GONE OUT INTO ALL THE EARTH,
AND THEIR WORDS TO THE ENDS OF THE WORLD."
(Romans 10:11–18)